Yes, Sir!
MR. PRESIDENT

Howie Franklin
with Mark Grady

Webster Falls Media

Books • Films

www.websterfalls.com

The stories in this book are based on the recollection of the author. Some details, specifics or names may have been changed or deleted in order to protect the privacy of those involved.

Published by Webster Falls Media LLC

www.websterfalls.com

First Edition

Library of Congress Control Number: 2015937638

ISBN (hardcover): 978-0-9816872-2-3

Printed in the USA

To Adam, now in the Wild Blue, too.

Acknowledgements

A great number of people have come and gone in my life. I owe all of them a debt for the way they have enriched my life. Trying to name all of them would be a book in itself, but I do want to single out some of them.

Chief Master Sergeant Charlie Palmer; dedicated to his family, the Air Force, his job, the crew of Air Force One and the President of the United States; was the one who hired me and gave me the opportunity to be part of the Air Force One family. For that I will be forever grateful.

The Presidential Pilots I worked for: Colonel Les McClelland, Colonel Bob Ruddick, and Colonel Danny Barr always had our backs. Colonel "Buzz" Buzzelli was the informal leader who kept the crew's antics on an even keel. Chief Master Sergeant Ozias Gray, with his subtle, wry sense of humor, always made sure the paperwork was done, not to mention our flight pay, flying hours and crew party finances. Chief Master Sergeant Kim Johnson made sure we were all well-informed and on track. It was my honor to be the Deputy to Chief Master Sergeant John Haigh while he was Chief Steward aboard Air Force One.

I would also like to thank all the Flight Attendants in the Air Force, the 89th Military Airlift Wing and the Flight Attendants and crew on Air Force One. I know what they do. I know how difficult it is at times and how rewarding it can be. I salute them for their dedication and hard work.

In addition to my Air Force family, I owe a huge debt of gratitude to my real family. From my wonder wife Linda to my fantastic children - Wayne, Cherie, Bobby, Lisa, Beth and Adam - they have certainly made my life a great one. They taught me a lot and are a great blessing.

Thanks to the co-author of this book, Mark Grady, for spending many hours with me capturing my stories and turning them into a real book.

In my new position as director of the Cape Fear Regional Jetport at Howie Franklin Field, I am honored to work with an airport board and staff that's second to none. To be in an entirely new career that is just as rewarding as my time on the president's plane makes me one extremely lucky and grateful guy.

- Howie Franklin
Oak Island, N.C.

I'm very grateful to Howie and Linda Franklin for selecting me to go on this adventure in bringing Howie's fantastic stories to life in this book.

While it has been one of the most challenging projects I've ever worked on, in the positive sense, it also has been one of the most rewarding.

Thank you to the many friends who always inspire and encourage me in every endeavor I take. Tom C. Freeman, Alnita Coulter, Carlton Vinson and Carl Jackson are just a few.

Always, I thank my great daughter and son, Kayla and Michael, just for being you.

- Mark Grady
Carolina Beach, N.C.

Foreword

As a history buff, I know some events in our country's history fall under the radar. There are many important and interesting occurrences that don't make the history books. Such is the case with Howie Franklin and his life's stories.

When William Jefferson Clinton was sworn into office as our 42nd president, he made the history books. That event meant Howie Franklin made history, too, by becoming the first U.S. Air Force flight attendant on Air Force One to serve five U.S. presidents.

Since Howie's retirement from the Air Force, I've had the chance to see Howie put his incredible people skills to work in the position he fills today as director of the Cape Fear Regional Airport in North Carolina. I've seen those skills before and during the times I was aboard Air Force One as a passenger. He gets things done and keeps the people he is serving happy.

Yes, Sir! Mr. President is a fast-moving adventure through Howie's life and the incredible, unpredictable turn of events that landed him on the president's plane, where he eventually worked his way up to Chief Steward.

You will be entertained by these stories and learn about a unique side of presidential life – life above 30,000 feet – that you don't normally observe.

- Bill Bennett
  Former Education Secretary to President Reagan and Drug Czar to President George H.W. Bush

Chapter One

It was in April of 1994 that I walked down the steps of Air Force One for the last time as Chief Steward on the President's plane. As I strolled across the ramp at Andrews Air Force Base, outside of Washington, I glanced back at the Boeing 747 and the huge letters "United States of America" boldly adorning the side of the airplane.

In reality, I had mixed emotions about the day. On one hand, I was excited about the next chapter of my life. I was heading to southeastern North Carolina to make a more stable life with my wife, Linda, who also served aboard Air Force One, and our son, Adam.

A new job awaited me as manager of a community airport in a great town, Southport. The decision to make that our home was not a difficult one. I was from Long Island, New York, while Linda was from North Carolina. We had visited both areas before deciding where to plant some roots. Long Island had pine trees, the ocean and was a beautiful place. Southport had pine trees, the ocean and was also a beautiful place. The dealmaker? In Southport, it was 72 degrees in February! That was easy.

My decision to retire from the Air Force and strike out on my new airport manager adventure was not perfect timing. President Clinton was in the early stages of his second term and was facing some scandals in the media. The Presidential Pilot of Air Force One did not want the President to make the wrong assumption about my departure. And since the Presidential Pilot was on leave at the time I was scheduled to leave Air Force One, he gave me an order.

"Don't tell the President you're leaving until I get back," he said. "I want to be there because I don't want him to think you're jumping ship on him."

So, here I was, on my last duty day aboard the President's plane and I could not tell him I was leaving. It was a little easier to avoid the issue since I had assigned another flight attendant to serve the President on that flight while I worked the staff.

Since I was under orders to keep mum with the President, one of the reflections that crossed my mind was a misconception many have about working on the plane. Some people believe it must be really difficult to work for the leader of the free world when he is on board.

In reality, the President was usually the easiest person to please on Air Force One. The staff? That sometimes was a different story. The President's staff is where the power is. The other regular passengers on board, the press, could also be tougher to please than the President.

Not all of my last-day reflections were serious. I also thought about the funny times that kept us sane during the really busy days. One of those memories centered around a running gag on board Air Force One. Diet Coke was a big seller on board. So, the ongoing joke was, "Give me five Diet Cokes and keep 'em rolling!"

Many of the memories that crossed my mind on that last day also involved my entire Air Force career, not just my many years on Air Force One. There had been quite a career before I had landed into the most important flight attendant job in the country.

What I had expected would be a simple job of food service in the Air Force had evolved quicker than I could ever imagine. Before I knew it I was working for some of the most powerful people in America. I had served five U.S. Presidents. Prior to working on Air Force One I had been on high-level, sometimes top-secret, missions with the top brass in the military. When the historic shuttle diplomacy missions were taking place in the Middle East involving then-Secretary of State Henry Kissinger, I was on the team.

In addition, flights aboard the President's plane also included passengers that were well-known celebrities and colorful news media people. I had served them all.

There were long duty times, sometimes over 50 hours at a time with little or no sleep. I had served nice people and not so nice ones. History was being made around me. And I had worked with some great people, having some good laughs along the way.

It's in reflection that you begin to see how everything in your life was always preparing you for the next phase. I was thinking about that on my last day walking away from Air Force One. I could have never imagined that a Long Island teenager working at a yacht club, serving the rich and sometimes famous, was actually in training to serve the most powerful men in the free world. But, now it all made sense. You joined the Air Force to see the World, and son, I got to see the World! In fact, the countries I haven't been to would be easier to name than the ones I have been to.

Yes, I was excited about my new future in North Carolina, but I also realized that up to this point my life had already been one hell of a ride. I think you'll agree.

Chapter Two

When I reflect on my life I'm amazed how everything, from where I grew up to the first jobs I had, was preparing me for the best noncommissioned officers' job the Air Force has to offer.

I grew up in Bayport, New York on Long Island. It was like growing up in Disneyland.

Since Long Island was what I knew, I thought everyone lived like we did. In fact, when most people would ask me in my young days where I was from I would say New York, thinking it was more sophisticated to be from the city than a small town. I would later learn it was really something to be from Bayport.

Not too long ago, I took my son, Adam, to Bayport to give him a tour of where I grew up. His first response was about something more common in small towns.

"What's with all the school crossing guards?" he asked.

"This is small town America," I said. "There are no buses. Kids walk to school."

While Bayport is a small town, it is big in one thing. Money.

The Roosevelts had an estate there, as did the Vanderbilts.

Life for me as a kid was pretty easy. My parents had married later than most people did. My father had returned home from World War II and had settled in before marrying my mother. She had retired after 20 years with the telephone company and my father had become the manager of the local Lincoln-Mercury dealership. I wasn't born until my mother was 42 years old.

As if Bayport wasn't fancy enough for a kid to grow up in, my summers were spent as close to paradise as you can get. My grandfather had built several homes across the bay on Fire Island. That's where I would spend every summer.

After school was out for the summer, I was on the ferry and headed for Fire Island. From the first day of summer vacation until I went back to school, I stayed in bare feet with T-shirts and bathing suits as my only attire. Going back to school was tough because I had to start wearing shoes again!

Fire Island is 35 miles long and is a half-mile wide at its widest point. Its proximity to New York City and the seclusion of being a barrier island had quickly earned it a reputation as the place to be for celebrities, especially in the area known as Ocean Beach. During the summer, I would share the playground with Chris Wallace, now of Fox News, and his brother. In fact, the first time I had ever heard a married couple in an argument was between Chris's father, Mike Wallace, of *60 Minutes* fame, and his wife, Buff Todd. During those days, Mike was the host of a talk show in New York.

Years later, Chris had become a White House correspondent and was on Air Force One.

"Remember going to Ocean Beach?" I asked him on the plane.

"Oh, yeah!" Chris said, obviously excited about the reminder.

"Well, I used to play with your brother at the playground."

That led to us reminiscing about summers at Ocean Beach on Fire Island.

Fire Island was always filled with celebrities during the summer. Of all the famous folks who came to our little slice of heaven, one really captured the hearts and imagination of all the young boys on the beach, including me. Marilyn Monroe.

The reason we knew all these people were on the island was because many of us boys had become young entrepreneurs serving these celebrities. Cars were not allowed on Fire Island. So, when the visitors arrived at Ocean Beach by ferry, there we were, with wagons dragging behind us, ready to transport their luggage from the ferry dock to their rented beach villa. We made good summer tip money. Since we had a front row seat to everyone coming and going on the island we knew when Marilyn would be there with Joe DiMaggio.

You didn't have to be a grown man to know that Marilyn was considered one sexy lady. In fact, rumor had it that she sunbathed in the nude while she was there. However, the house they rented was surrounded by huge hedge bushes, preventing you from seeing into the grounds. When we would walk by the place, it would drive us young guys crazy just knowing that Marilyn Monroe could be on the other side of those bushes, sans clothes, soaking up the sun and infecting our imagination. To this day, when I see or smell those big hedge bushes, I think of Marilyn Monroe.

By the time I was working age, about 16, I landed a job that would have me serving the rich and famous on a big scale during the summer months. It was at a place called Talisman Yacht Club.

During its heyday, Talisman Yacht Club was the place to be on Fire Island. It attracted the famous and the wealthy. The place featured 16 cabanas, four houses and beautiful gardens, all done Japanese style. There was even a fenced-in paddle tennis court at the club.

Talisman Yacht Club was the place for the jet-set crowd of the 60s. Baby Jane Holzer, with her famous long, blond hair, and her Manhattan real-estate developer husband, Lenny, were frequently among the average of 65 people who would be weekend guests. Another regular guest was Bill Cullen, the original host of *The Price is*

Right. The Coleman family, of the camping supply company fame, were regulars. Ahmet Ertegun, president of Atlantic Record Company, would bring Ray Charles there early in his career. Carol Channing was a frequent visitor, too. They were guests of the members, the jetsetters. It was not unusual for counts and princes to be guests. The dock would fly flags representing the home countries of the yacht club visitors.

I learned some important people lessons by being around the famous movie stars and politicians that invaded our island in the summer. I discovered they were real people. They feel. They care. And while society tends to put them on a pedestal, they are actually no different than the rest of us. In fact, the people I worked for and saw on Fire Island were actually more wealthy and powerful than many of the passengers I would eventually serve on Air Force One. That fact would make my life a little easier when it came to working on the President's plane.

While Japanese was the primary motif at Talisman Yacht Club, the food featured dishes from all over the world that were prepared by award-winning chefs. They became important, big-time mentors to me.

The first chef I worked for was a Hungarian Jewish lady who had been a top chef in Florida at the Fontainebleau. She had been a prisoner of the Nazis in World War II and had the tattoo on her arm to prove it. Working for her was an amazing education. In hearing her talk about her past, I was always amazed that she worked at Talisman because it was managed by a German gentleman.

One story in particular sent chills down my spine. She told me about a day she was being made to march by the Germans. As they began to spray the people with machine gun fire, she fell in the mud among the fallen bodies. The only reason she survived was because the Germans thought she was already dead.

The next chef I worked for was Italian-American. Then, I worked for a Turkish lady who liked the other boys on the staff and me simply because of our appetite.

"These are good boys! They eat!" she would say.

Chapter Three

Early in my work with food at the resort, I became involved in acquiring the food we would prepare in the restaurant. Everything was purchased retail. We would take the water taxi over to the main island and go into the stores with the weekend menu. We would buy what we needed to prepare for a Friday night dinner, Saturday breakfast, Saturday lunch, Saturday dinner, Sunday breakfast and lunch, and for a light dinner on Sunday since many of the guests would head out Sunday afternoon. We would box up what we bought and take it via the water taxi back to the yacht club to be put away.

I was certainly unaware of it at the time, but I was doing exactly what I would be doing on Air Force One. It was real-life training.

If you were to describe my main work on Air Force One as steward, it was basically as food and beverage manager. Part of that meant I was responsible for buying what we needed for each mission with the President. Since we were serving the leader of the free world, security was paramount. If someone intended to do harm to the president, one way would be to poison the food he consumed. So we had a system in place to ensure his safety that was very similar to the way we purchased food at the Talisman Yacht Club.

Once a menu for a flight was put together and approved by the White House, we donned our civilian clothes and went to the grocery store. We would rotate stores where we shopped and would never identify ourselves as the crew from Air Force One. We would pay for the food and return to wherever the plane happened to be on that mission and begin the process of preparing meals and storing what would be needed later.

It wasn't just the food where safety was a concern. Anything the president, the crew or guests on board would put in their mouth had to be purchased carefully. From candy and chewing gum to toothpaste and mouthwash, they were all gathered using the same security measures used in getting food. Our system insured everything brought on board had been purchased secretly and without any system you could track. If the bad man doesn't know your plan they can't plan for you.

In today's post 9/11 environment, security is even tighter. After all, Air Force One is not another skyscraper. There is nothing else like it and the bad guys would love to hit that plane.

The last chef I worked for at Talisman was a man named George Garofellow. Everyone called him "Ferouk" because his big handlebar moustache made him look like the Egyptian King Ferouk.

His stories left me fascinated with the big world there was beyond Long Island, New York. I thought I was going to get the chance to see the world from aboard a Greek freighter. After all, one of the owners of Talisman Yacht Club was Harry Theodore Acropolis, the owner of Greek International Lines, and I had been given the opportunity to go to sea and work for him.

I was going to see the world alright. But, it was going to be in an entirely different way than a Greek ship. On the other side of the globe, there was something going on that was called by politicians a "police action" or "conflict." The rest of us called it war. It was happening in a place that had become a household word and a regular part of the nightly news – Vietnam.

Ever since I turned 18, the draft was on my mind. I had hit 20 years old and Uncle Sam was about to take me out of the luxury of Long Island and change my life forever.

Chapter Four

Just as I feared, Uncle Sam sent me a kind notice, via a uniformed member of the United States Postal Service. Mine came two years after I had obtained my draft card. In most cases a draft notice would tell you to report for a physical and to take a battery of tests. Then, you would go home and wait for further orders on what to do next.

In my case, as well as the case of four of my friends, the draft notice was worded a bit more urgently than what we expected. It read, "IMMEDIATE INDUCTION AFTER PHYSICAL."

The five of us sat on the front porch of my home pondering what was happening to us.

"What are we going to do?" we all seemed to ask in unison.

It was 1965. The anti-war movement was not yet in full swing, but film from the front line was showing up on the national TV newscasts.

Growing up in an exclusive small town, we had been shielded from even simple unpleasant parts of life. Now, reality was staring us right in the face.

14

I decided I needed to talk to an Army recruiter. When I walked into the recruiting center, I was welcomed by a big sergeant. My respect for the military was always high and I was impressed by the man before me in his uniform. But, I was hoping to minimize my risks.

"Sir, the way I understand it, if I go the drafted route it's two years," I said. "If I enlist, it's three years. If I score high on my tests, do I have any chance of getting into the career field that I want?"

I was obviously talking with an honest man. He said, "Son, in the Army no matter how high you test you always test highest in the infantry."

The honest sergeant convinced me the Army would probably not be the best choice.

When I regrouped with my friends on Long Island, we now had feedback from some other friends who had already been in the military. One of them, who had served in the Army, backed up my decision about that branch not being a good choice.

"It ain't pretty," he said.

We talked with a guy on leave who served in the Marine Corps. After hearing his description, we concluded those guys lived in a helmet. They ate out of a helmet and shaved out of their helmet. Yet, the Marines kept telling them how great they were, which I guess was okay if that's how you had to live. But my friends and I concluded, "That's not good."

When we turned to friends who were in the U.S. Navy, they said, "The romanticism of being on a ship, at sea, wears off really fast, in about five days."

That left one branch of the service. Since I had a cousin in the Air Force, I told my friends, "You know, I don't think those guys carry guns."

Many years later, one of the passengers aboard Air Force One during the George H.W. Bush administration was a Marine Corps Colonel named Charles C. Krulak. He went on to become a General and the Commandant of the Marine Corps.

"Howie, why did you choose the Air Force?"

"Well, sir, in 1965 I discovered that the United States Air Force was the only branch of the military where the enlisted man is not the primary resource being shot at."

Col. Krulak laughed, but I was telling the truth. I may have been only 20 years old when I enlisted, but I had developed one good skill. I could listen.

Since I had to go into New York City to visit with the Air Force Recruiter in 1965, I decided to kill two birds with one stone. First, I signed up for the Air Force and asked to be placed in food service. Since I already had experience in working with food at the yacht club, I figured it would be a piece of cake. Plus, I thought just maybe the Air Force might teach me a few more culinary tricks.

After signing on the dotted line, I made my way into an exclusive part of Manhattan where I was escorted to the top floor, skyscraper office of one Harry Theodore Acropolis. Remarkably, the owner of Greek International Lines let me in. I still had that offer to go to sea in my mind.

I told him about my plan. I would do my few years in the Air Force and then return to New York to take a job working on one of his Greek passenger ships. The man was very kind and friendly, despite the fact I now know my plans were not on his list of the most important issues of the day. I left his office feeling confident I had my life all planned out. Boy, was I about to learn plans don't always mean a lot.

Chapter Five

Obviously, the four friends who had pondered the best branch of the military to sign up with all agreed with me on my choice of the Air Force. The five of us joined at the same time and, before we knew it, we were on our way to basic training at Lackland Air Force Base in San Antonio, Texas.

I kept in mind some advice about basic training given to me by a good friend. He said, "Try not to let anyone know who you are. Don't volunteer to do anything, just do what they tell you to do."

I thought I was good at that.

One August afternoon it was about 110 degrees in San Antonio. Because of the heat, we had been ordered by our T.I. (Training Instructor) to stay in the barracks. Most of the fellow enlistees were right out of high school while the five of us were all around 20 years old. So, we had a bit more life and work experience than the other guys. Because of that difference we would occasionally find ourselves with a self-imposed challenge no other recruit would ever consider.

In order to instill us with some discipline, many things we had been accustomed to in our great life on Long Island were now not part of the Air Force's plan for us in training. This included one thing we took for granted back home – a nice, cold Coca-Cola.

One of my friends who had enlisted with me, Jack, gave me the challenge.

"Howie, why don't you go over to the patio area and get us some Cokes?"

There were several problems surrounding his request. First, I've already mentioned that Cokes were not on the regular menu for airmen in training. Then, we had our orders to stay in the barracks. The patio with the soda machine was across the grounds. There was also a problem of trying to secretly transport the bottles back to the barracks since we were not supposed to have anything in our uniform pockets.

On rare occasions, we would be given permission to visit the patio, but only as a group, known as a "flight." Today was not one of those occasions.

With the mercury about to bust out of the top of the thermometer, along with the fact that this particular soda machine featured the small, six-ounce bottle of Coke that everyone was convinced tasted better than any other size, I was inspired to take on Jack's challenge. I left the barracks with the patio as my destination.

I bought one Coke from the machine and drank it down right there so there would be one less bottle I had to transport across the grounds in my pockets. It tasted great.

After polishing mine off, I bought two more, put them in my pockets and started making my way back to the barracks. Unbeknownst to me, another T.I. had spotted me strolling along with the tops of two Coca-Cola bottles swaying out of my pockets. He was salivating over this great discovery and could not wait to intercept the new airman on the block.

"Airman Franklin, Report!"

I jumped to attention immediately.

"Airman Franklin, reporting as ordered, SIR!"

That's when the screaming commenced.

"Airman Franklin, you know the rules! What an outrage! What makes you think it's okay to walk around with two soda bottles hanging out of your uniform pockets?"

Still firmly at attention, I said, "Sir, I'm a dipshit. I don't know how to drink a soda properly and until I learn how to drink a soda properly I have to walk around with these soda bottles and tell everybody I'm a dipshit."

Obviously believing I was under the orders of my regular T.I., a man who had occasional bouts of over-consuming alcohol, he shouted out, "Well, carry on Airman!"

He loved it. I had made his day.

I bet you ten dollars to a doughnut that he went to the club with his buddies that night and told them, "You should have seen the dipshit I saw today!"

My friend Jack and I sat back in our barracks and could care less what that guy thought of us. We were enjoying our covertly obtained Coca-Colas.

Believe it or not, the way I handled that incident got me through a lot of other situations in the Air Force. Whenever I was dealing with difficult people who thought they were better than I was, I would simply ask myself, "Do I have my soda bottles?"

To this day, I've used that mindset to deal with office politics in my work. Thank God for soda bottles. There are times when I think we all could use a few of them in our pockets.

Of the five of us Long Island guys who had enlisted in the Air Force together, I was the only one who survived the first four years of the Air Force. The rest eventually washed out. Ironically, they all were the ones who had expressed an interest in making it their career, while I was the one with plans to work on Greek cruise ships after a few years. I guess they could have used my philosophy of soda bottles.

When my basic training days at Lackland AFB were coming to an end, I began to wonder what the Air Force was going to do with me. Finally, I got my assignment and was happy to see they were placing me in the work area I wanted - food service.

I turned to my fellow enlistee friend and said, "I got *what* I wanted, but I don't know *where* I'm going."

He looked at my assignment.

"There it is right there," he said. "S.D.A.K."

"S.D.A.K.? Where's that?"

"South Dakota," he said.

Despite the San Antonio heat, a quick chill went down my spine. I thought about how many times I had heard weather forecasts that began with "bad weather coming down from the Dakotas."

Before the day was over, I knew exactly where I was headed. Rapid City, South Dakota. Specifically, Ellsworth Air Force Base.

Chapter Six

With my basic training behind me, I was now enroute to Ellsworth Air Force Base. I tried to avoid thinking about the weather that awaited me there. Instead, I focused on a rumor I had heard about Rapid City. It was, "There's a woman behind every tree." Little did I know there were hardly any trees around Ellsworth AFB.

I can best describe my first days in South Dakota as grim. Here I was, a guy who spent summers in the luxury of Fire Island serving what I thought was a large group of the rich and famous who vacationed there. Quickly, my definition of a "large group" had changed. Now, I was feeding 2,000 people every meal AND cleaning up after them. In the Air Force, the cooks handle KP, too.

Most of my first days at Ellsworth were spent in this monster of a dish washing machine known as the "Clipper." As I cleaned the dishes, pots and pans that served a couple of thousand hungry members of the U.S. Air Force, I could not help but think, "This is my career?" Like I said, grim.

Desperate for an escape from the routine, four of us decided to make a 70-mile trip to Spearfish, South Dakota where they were holding a dance. We had spent a long, hard day working in the dining hall, but needed the break. After the dance, on the way back to base, we were involved in a serious car accident. All of us were injured and taken to a hospital.

At first I thought I was the luckiest of the group, because I was the first one released. My hospital freedom was short-lived. The next morning, one of my knees had swollen to the size of a basketball. Before I knew it, I was back in the hospital only to become the last one released. I had cartilage replaced in my knees and it would be a three-month recovery in the hospital.

One day during my hospital stay, a blizzard came through the area. And sports fans, when a blizzard comes through South Dakota, they don't mess around. They were masterpieces of blizzards.

The roads had become so impassable the cooks could not make it to the hospital. Quickly, word got out that this one-striper Airman named Franklin was a food service guy. Another man in the hospital was a staff sergeant with twenty years in the Air Force, also in food service.

They rounded us both up and said, "Hey, you guys are food service. You've got to feed the hospital." It was a big hospital.

Still confined to crutches when I walked, I hobbled down to the kitchen. The staff sergeant greeted me with, "We can't do it. There are locks on the freezer and the refrigerator."

I rumbled through the kitchen and found a meat cleaver. Wham! I used it to break the locks off of both units and we went to work.

With some limited help from a few medics, we pulled it off. We fed everyone in the hospital. We even prepared the special meals for patients on restricted diets.

Impressed with my work, by the time I was discharged from the hospital the hospital commander had given me a raise in rank. So, I returned to work on base with a higher rank than I had when I left to go to the dance. My soda bottle philosophy had paid off again.

The only ones not impressed with my new rank were my friends who had gone with me to the dance. They were in shock that a guy could get a higher rank while hospitalized.

Not only did I return with a higher rank, I also returned to find I had a job I liked quite a bit better than spending my days at the grim Clipper. Now, I was assigned in Ration Breakdown. In this part of food service, rations would come in from the Commissary. We would then divide them up to be shipped to the missile sites in refrigerated trucks.

Large missile sites were like their own small cities. They had big crews and officers at these important parts of our nation's defense. At these sites, they didn't eat in a dining hall like most bases. They ate like they would at home.

On one shift in Ration Breakdown, I got word that I would be involved in a shipment going to Guam. It was the best news I had received since arriving in South Dakota. To say I didn't want to be in Rapid City was an understatement. In fact, not too long after arriving, I made a visit to a Navy recruiter in a desperate attempt to change services.

"When you wrap up your time in the Air Force, we'd love to have you," the recruiter said.

"I don't think you understand," I said. "I want out now."

With that failed attempt behind me, finding out I was headed to the warmth of the South Pacific was fantastic news. Knowing my overwhelming desire to head towards Guam was mostly based on temperature, I thought it would be nice to get some feedback on what Guam was really like. I'd get a first-hand assessment from a friend I had met in the Air Force named Freddy Grey.

I was drawn to Freddy because I could relate to him. Like me, he was a New Englander. He was from Jersey City, New Jersey and carried the accent to prove it.

One day, I happened to be in Dining Hall Four at Ellsworth AFB and witnessed the Jersey attitude display itself through Freddy, a four-year, three-striper. He was mopping the floor when a first sergeant came in and sat down to drink a cup of coffee.

"You know, you've done real good, Airman Grey," the first sergeant said. "You've made three stripes and we're proud of you in the Air Force. We'd like to see you re-enlist."

Freddy stopped working and leaned on his mop.

"Sarge, when I came to this base four years ago, you know what my first job was?" he asked in his strong, New Jersey accent. "Mopping the floor in Dining Hall Four. I tell you what. You give me $35,000 and a new Cadillac and I'll extend for a week. I'd rather be back on the block selling pencils on a street corner in Newark than stay in this chicken outfit."

Freddy then went back to mopping.

At one point, Freddy had spent some brief time in Guam.

"How was Guam?" I asked him.

"I couldn't wait to get back to South Dakota!" Freddy said.

My first reaction was, "Damn, what have I gotten myself into now?" Fortunately, I would get some better feedback and advice from another airman I had befriended in Rapid City.

"When you go to Guam, try to get in the in-flight kitchen," he said. "Don't go to the dining halls. It's terrible, like slave labor. Do what you have to and get in the in-flight kitchen."

"What do I have to do to get in the in-flight kitchen?"

"You've got to drive a military vehicle and you deliver flight lunches to the crews of the B-52s that are bombing North Vietnam."

This guy seemed to know what he was talking about. It made sense. However, there was one big obstacle standing in the way of me getting on the in-flight kitchen crew once I arrived on Guam. In order to drive a military vehicle you had to have a military driver's license with certain endorsements. That was something I didn't have.

While many may consider food service a low-class job in the Air Force, it did have its advantages. One was that everybody liked you because everybody liked to eat. Food could be powerful currency in the U.S. Air Force and I had learned to use it in a way that would make Radar O'Reilly on M*A*S*H very proud. I decided it was time to put those skills to work now. So, I called the man on base in charge of giving the tests and issuing Air Force driver's licenses and endorsements. I explained my situation to him and asked if there was any way of expediting the process before I went to Guam.

"What kind of food do you have prepared over there, Franklin?" he asked me.

"Sir, I have three fried chickens here now."

"Bring 'em on over," he said.

I assumed that would be payment for expediting the process. I had no idea that I was actually trading three chickens for an official Air Force driver's license.

Not only did the recipient of my three, government-reallocated chickens give me a military driver's license in return, he gave me one that had almost every endorsement you could think of. I could even have driven one of the huge, missile carrying trucks! Now that's three valuable chickens!

The benefits of the chicken-for-license exchange did not end there. Just after my barter arrangement, word came down through normal channels that Airman Franklin had received the highest test score on the military driver's license exam in the history of the base! I never saw an exam, much less take one.

In the words of the infomercial announcer, "And that's not all!"

The man who ran food services on base was a rather rough, tattooed warrant officer. He saw this event as a chance to get some attention for his usually-ignored unit. So, what did he do? He put together a huge ceremony to honor me for my history-making grade on the driver's test. While everyone stood around me, singing my praises, the warrant officer was proud. That made one of us. I was scared the truth might come out.

The turn of events had changed my perspective. I was now wondering whether the most valuable items in the Air Force were soda bottles or chickens.

About a week after the All-Hail-Airman-Franklin ceremony, I was on the crew loading ration trucks in the middle of the night. A tech-sergeant named Pappy Jordan, who was from Atlanta, was with me.

"Airman Franklin, you've got that driver's license now, so why don't you go and pull that ration truck over here to help us out," Pappy ordered.

"Yes, sir!"

Freezing in the 30-degree-below-zero weather, I make my way over to the truck. I climbed in, found the key and started it up. For the next fifteen minutes I tried to figure out how the thing worked. There was this big gearshift knob, but no clutch. Nothing I tried seemed to work.

Most of the fifteen minutes were actually spent trying to get the guts to go tell this tech-sergeant that I didn't have the first clue how this truck works. Finally, I got the nerve, got out of the truck and confessed.

"What??!!" he shouted. "We just had a big ceremony for you! And you're saying you can't drive that truck!"

Since I was already in confession, I went on.

"Pappy, it cost me three chickens for that driver's license."

Lucky for me, he laughed and said, "Who didn't know that?"

Pappy had obviously used the food-for-needs system in his work, too.

30

Whether I could actually drive a truck or not, I did have my newly-acquired military driver's license with me when I launched out into the wild blue yonder from South Dakota. Destination: Guam. I was headed to work with the in-flight kitchen crew.

Chapter Seven

It turns out that both of the people at Ellsworth AFB giving me feedback about Guam were right. My friend recommending me make the switch to in-flight kitchen duty was right. I liked the job a lot better than working in the dining halls. However, Freddy Gray was right, too. Just like him, I hated Guam. The island was pretty, but that was it.

There were really no women to meet on Guam. That led to most single military people wasting away their off hours by drinking. Also, it was Guam that really made me homesick. Being in South Dakota was a long way from home, but that was nothing like being on the other side of the globe.

I became homesick on Guam, big time. When the holidays rolled around, hearing the Christmas music made me mad; mainly at myself. I realized I had taken a lot of things for granted back home, especially family. I had not treated Christmas with the importance I should have back on Long Island.

Another big difference between South Dakota and Guam was that it brought me closer to what was happening in Vietnam. I was seeing the Air Force at work in its bombing runs.

Since my new job required feeding the flight crews on the B-52s, I was aware of the bombing schedule. I knew how much time it took to get a bomber over North Vietnam and was amazed at the strategy and the timing. In fact, most everyone back home was aware of the cease-fires that popped up around Christmas, Easter and other holidays. The Air Force had timed it out with such precision that the bombs were falling again within a minute of the cease-fires coming to an end.

Despite the misery of missing home and the loneliness on Guam, I still tried to make the most of it and did the best job I could. So, I tried to keep a smile on my face and share a happy thought when I interacted with the flight crews. As a result, they liked me.

One day, a flight crew came up to me. One of them said, "We'd like to cross-train you to be a flight attendant."

That job had never crossed my mind at this point. I was actually enjoying the in-flight kitchen work, and the hours and conditions were certainly better than working in the dining halls.

The only thing that made me initially curious about their offer was wondering if it could mean a ticket off of Guam. I was approaching nine months on the island.

"What would I have to do?" I asked them.

"We checked your records and the only thing you would have to do is extend your time in the Air Force an additional eight months, after your four years is up."

It didn't take me long to respond to that one.

"I'm sorry. I'm out."

Anyone who went past four years in the Air Force was considered a "lifer." There was also a much less attractive name for someone going past that mark – a "puke." I wanted to get out and go home.

They tried one more approach, and unbeknownst to me at the time, it was going to change my life.

"Let us just take you on one flight and see how you like it."

My introductory flight into the world of being an Air Force flight attendant, in early 1967, did show me there were some advantages to the job. Instead of an official uniform, I simply wore a white shirt with black pants and black shoes. I didn't have to wear a tie because it was so hot on Guam.

I boarded the KC-97, known in the civilian world as the Boeing Stratocrusier. It was actually a derivative of the B-29 and the predecessor to the Boeing 707.

Our 25 passengers on board the plane included full colonels and a general, but not just any general. This general was the man in charge of the Strategic Air Command (SAC) in

Southeast Asia. It was a ten-hour flight from Guam to our destination, Okinawa.

There was some good news awaiting me when we landed. I found out my best friend, who I had grown up with and gone to high school with on Long Island, was stationed on Okinawa. He was in the Marine Corps and was the only enlisted Marine on the island that lived in off-base housing with his wife. His name was Jimmy Otto.

When I called his number, a girl answered the phone with a wonderful southern accent. It was his wife and she was from Nashville, Tennessee.

"Hi, my name is Howie Franklin."

Before I could say anything else, she said, "I've heard all about you! Jimmy is out right now, but tell me where you are and he'll call you as soon as he gets in."

It wasn't long before my old friend called and told me he was coming to pick me up. When he arrived, I did a double take. He was driving a Jeepster. Classic car aficionados will know the Jeepster is a cross between a sports car and a Jeep. This one had a huge Chevrolet engine in it and very nice rims. My first thought was how did this enlisted guy put together the money to buy this thing and live in off-base housing, too? I'd soon find out.

Jimmy pulled up wearing black jeans and a T-shirt. He had the infamous Marine Corps bulldog tattooed on one arm and "Mom" tattooed on the other. This big, red-headed Irish guy was on

Guam to basically be re-introduced to society after having spent a long time in the jungles of Vietnam with a recon group. Those guys had it rough. Many even had to eat snakes to survive. So, they were sent to Okinawa after their time in Nam to re-acclimate themselves into normal life.

Jimmy started right away filling me in on his life.

"Guess what? I'm married," he said.

"Yea, I heard."

"I married a stripper. They call her 'Big Red.'"

As we continued our drive around Okinawa, Jimmy pulled out his wallet and began showing me photos of his wife taken in front of beer joints where she was "performing."

He said his wife was making about $350 a week, much more than his Marine Corps income, and he was loansharking the money out. That explained the Jeepster, I thought.

After updating me on what had been happening with him, Jimmy turned to me.

"What can I do for you?" he asked.

Impressed by my old friend's turn of fate, I said, "Fix me up!"

Next thing you know I'm being introduced to one of Big Red's colleagues in the stripping business. Her stage name was Marie Diamond, but since she was a petite blond that everyone thought looked like a doll, her nickname was "Dolly."

For the rest of that visit, and every time I ended up on Okinawa in the near future after that time, I'd have dinner with Dolly and we would hang out.

Late into the night of our first meeting I finally had to ask.

"I know your real name isn't Dolly and it's not Marie Diamond, so what is your real name?"

"My real name is Doris Kilwalski and I'm from Camden, New Jersey."

Here I was on the other side of the world sitting with a Jersey girl.

Chapter Eight

My first 24 hours on Okinawa were spent primarily with Doris, aka Dolly. The next day I had to report back to the KC-97 for a two-hour flight to carry the general and his colleagues to Taipei, Taiwan.

Once we were airborne, the fact I had not slept for almost two days was catching up with me. When I approached the general to serve him some coffee, I was being extra careful because my hands were a bit shaky from the fatigue. He noticed it and looked up only to see me looking back with bloodshot eyes.

"Hey, Franklin?" the general said.

"Yes, sir."

"Nice eyes."

I immediately jumped into defense mode.

"I wasn't drinking, sir. I just didn't get any sleep."

"Did you have a good time?"

"I had a great time, sir."

The general smiled.

This brief exchange with top military brass on board the plane was one of the things that was changing my perspective about being a flight attendant, even if it did mean eight more months tagged on to the four years I had already signed up for. In ground-based food service, I was in a group I did not feel was well-managed at the time. There was consistent vulgarity among that crew and we all felt unappreciated and disrespected. Now, here I was checking out the world of an Air Force flight attendant and things were different. A lot different.

The flight crew seemed to really enjoy what they were doing. The flight attendants were treated well and seemed to be respected. And, here I was exchanging pleasantries with not just any general, but the guy in charge of SAC in Southeast Asia; and he seemed to like me. This was starting to be a little like an airborne version of Talisman Yacht Club. Not quite, but close.

When we landed in Taipei, we ended up there for five days. Compared to Guam, it was a great experience. The flight crew would all go out and eat dinner every evening and then browse around. I could spend a long time talking about what an incredible five days I had in Taiwan.

Within a short time of arriving in Taipei, the flight crew started asking me the same question on a frequent basis. It became almost a running gag.

"Son, you gonna sign up?" they would ask.

"Nah, not me," I'd say. "This is pretty good, but not me."

In reality, if this Taipei trip was any indication then the flight attendant thing was really looking good. I had always heard some advice growing up that I frequently share with young people today. Find something you love so much you are willing to do it for nothing and get paid for it. This flight attendant introduction had been the closest I had come to that in the Air Force. But, my internal dialog was still arguing with itself.

What are you thinking? You hate the Air Force! You want even more time in this?!!? Not really, but, then again, I'm kind of liking this part of it.

When our flight returned to Guam, the flight crew went right to work trying to encourage me to go to personnel and make the switch. I was still reluctant. Then, they hit with some deal-breaking information I didn't know about.

"Either way, in or out, you need to go to personnel anyway to get your per diem for the trip."

"What?"

I had just learned another great advantage of being an Air Force flight attendant. You got paid extra just for making the trip! I was amazed. After those amazing five days in Taipei, I felt like I should be paying *them* for the trip! I was going to get $28 a day for being on a flight from Guam to Okinawa, and then from Okinawa to Taiwan and back to Guam, including the five days in Taipei.

If that wasn't enough to make me happy, I also found out that if I made the switch to become a flight attendant that I would not only get the per diem, I'd also receive monthly flight pay.

I marched into the personnel office, filled out the paperwork to get my per diem and then said, "Sign me up!"

Airman Franklin was now a U.S. Air Force flight attendant.

Chapter Nine

All of us have those pivotal life-changing moments. One of the most significant ones for me came when I made the decision to switch to flight attendant duty. My entire perspective had changed. I had gone from despising the Air Force to absolutely loving my job.

This change of heart even convinced me to extend my time on Guam, a place I had initially hated, just because I had begun to spend most of my time on trips. I enjoyed those adventures so much that many of those days would stay in my mind as more enjoyable than the years I would later spend aboard Air Force One.

One of my earlier flights in my new work had me serving a three-star general who had an impressive family history of service to the military. One of his ancestors had been a general in the Confederate Army, while another had served in the Union Army with the same rank. His father had been a general and he was slotted to take over SAC in Omaha. He was from Georgia and they all had been graduates of West Point.

I was cleaning up in the galley during the flight when the general and the flight engineer, named Cliff Kershaw, came up to me.

"Howie, how's it going?" the general asked. "Do you like what you're doing?

"Yes, sir, I like it very much."

"I've never had service this good," the general said.

Apparently my past in working with the jet set crowd at Talisman Yacht Club was paying off. While most of the other flight attendants had received all of their training Air Force style, I had experience preparing food and serving people before I ever signed up. I could make anything from a rack of lamb to a New York deli-style sandwich and I enjoyed doing it. The people on the plane thought it was great and the general was going on and on about me only to be interrupted by Cliff Kershaw.

"General, we have one problem with Airman Franklin," Kershaw said. "When we go to Japan, we have to sneak him into the NCO club because he doesn't have enough rank to get in."

The general promoted me so I could go to the club. This job was getting better by the minute. I had been promoted while I was a patient in the hospital in South Dakota and now I was being promoted to staff sergeant after a brief discussion in the galley of an airplane. These two promotions had come in less than three years. That was unheard of in the Air Force.

The change of fortune did not just come with the change in rank. At one point, I had to move from where I was staying on Guam. The base commander asked me where I would like to live.

"Sir, the closer I am to the flight kitchen the easier it is for me to do my job."

Unbelievably, he assigned me to live in the VIP quarters usually reserved for the chief master sergeant. The surroundings were great and the place included a refrigerator that was always stocked with beer. I had a deal with a Filipino man who worked on base. Anytime I wanted a beer, I put 15 cents in the cup. I think he was buying them for ten cents, so I was always stocked. A win-win for him and me, and this time it didn't involve trading chickens.

Life was pretty easy. I had three sets of clothes. I would return from a trip and throw my dirty clothes on the floor before I hit the shower. I would take a set of clean clothes and put them in my hang-up bag, all ready for my next trip. The next day I would hit the cleaners and pick up my third set of clothes, cleaned and ready to go in the cycle and put my most recent dirty clothes in the cleaners.

While life on Guam had improved, my trips had taken me into an incredible life adventure.

It had become typical for me to return from a flight on Thursday night. On Friday I would attend a briefing. On Saturday morning, we would be in the air serving guys on a flight to Taipei for five days of R & R.

The only difference between the passengers on board and me was that I had just been in Taipei last week and I'm getting paid $28 a day to go back! While I certainly worked on the plane during the flight there and back, when I was in Taipei, waiting to bring the R & R group back to Guam, I lived a pretty elegant life.

If that wasn't the life of Riley, once a month we had another routine that was incredible.

Around the 29th of each month we would take a B-52 crew on its way to Vietnam and another group of men heading for R & R on a flight to Hong Kong. We would all spend the night there and the next day we would take the B-52 crew on to Saigon. We would drop the B-52 crew off, pick up a load of ceramic, Vietnamese-made elephants and fly on to Bangkok, Thailand, where we would stay for three days.

Whatever you've heard about Bangkok is true, and more so.

An airman friend of mine, Frank, and I ventured into a Bangkok massage parlor. They would give you a complete bath, scrubbing you from head to toe, and wash your hair. Then came a manicure and pedicure. It was such a luxurious experience that rumor had it Frank and I would take advantage of their services three times a day when we were in town. I neither confirm nor deny that rumor. I will say Frank and I were definitely the cleanest guys in Bangkok.

During the three-day visit, I also had a "top secret mission" to perform. On each trip I was given a check by the officer's wives' gift shop back on Guam, sometimes written for as much as $10,000. My mission was to go to James' Jewelers in Bangkok and buy jewelry for the gift shop. Plus, they would pay me to do this! I was the lowest ranked guy on the crew and I was buying stuff for the officer's wives' gift shop. I was an NCO in the Air Force and I don't think it was even legal for them to get me to do this. All I can say is, thank God for the statute of limitations.

After our three days in Bangkok were up, we were airborne again, back to Bien Hoa in Vietnam to pick up the B-52 crew and fly back to Hong Kong to spend the night. The next morning, the B-52 crew and the passengers we had left in Hong Kong for R & R were back on board. The flight plan called for refueling the plane in the Philippines.

That was the plan, but it never worked out that way. In the two years I was repeating these trips, the airplane never made it through the Philippines fuel stop without "breaking down."

To fully understand the importance of this story, you have to remember that the Air Force had a strictly-enforced 16-hour duty day. If you had been on duty for more than 16 hours, you were not allowed to fly. Period.

These "maintenance issues" would frequently be the result of a crew chief crawling down into the nose of the airplane, just after landing in the Philippines, to spray hydraulic fluid down the nose gear. When we stopped at the ramp, the refueling crew would spot all of this fluid "leaking."

They would say, "We have to write this up for maintenance to check out."

This meant the airplane was grounded, which usually only lasted for about one hour. But, wouldn't you know it, that hour put us past that 16-hour duty time which meant we were "stranded" in the Philippines for the night. I never knew which previous NCOs had created this system, but I always admired them.

Once we knew we had to spend the night I made a routine call to this hotel compound called the Marisaw Manor, just outside Clark Air Force Base. When they answered, I always had the same message.

"The Guam flyers are in town. Please pick us up in about 30 minutes."

By the way, when I identified myself there I did not use my name, Howie. In that area of the South Pacific, I quickly learned that "Howie" was a derogatory, racial slur towards a white man. So, everyone in that part of the world would call me Frankie. So, my routine call and request to the Marisaw Manor was always met with, "Yes, sir, Mr. Frankie!"

While our flight crew was intimately familiar with the "Philippines Refueling System," our passengers were not. They were patiently waiting in the terminal wondering what was going on and why they were being delayed.

Before they could get too concerned, a bus would pull up to the terminal, load them and their baggage, along with us, and take us to Marisaw Manor. Any anxiety they had about the delay was quickly eased when they found a nice, well-prepared buffet all laid out for them at the hotel. They would also hear an announcement.

"Attention all Guam flyers, special transportation will leave in one hour to take you downtown for shopping."

Since I was already a regular part of the Philippines maintenance delays, I passed on the shopping trips. I was more interested in getting some rest. So, I'd stay at the hotel and make a call to complete a routine, personal mission I had created. The call went to a Filipino friend and I would ask for my usual order of ten "Lazy Susans."

Most people remember the rotating Lazy Susan, once popular on dinner tables. The ones I would buy in the Philippines were wood with a hand-carved pineapple in the center. They were very popular back on Guam.

When my order arrived at the hotel, I would hand my friend a hundred dollar bill. The next day, they were on the flight with me back to Guam where I would sell them for $15 each. However, word eventually came down that I had to up my price to at least $20 because the officer's wives' gift shop had them marked for

$26 and they didn't want that much competition. American capitalism was alive and well for me in the U.S. Air Force.

One day I was on a flight to Japan with the three-star General Gillam on board. During the flight, he said, "Howie, we know you'll make a good master sergeant one day."

"Sir, I'd rather make a better civilian," I said, still sticking with my original plan of getting out and heading home when my time was up.

The general didn't take my response to heart.

"Well, I'm going to pull some strings and see if I can get you into the 89th," the general said.

The 89th is the Wing of the U.S. Air Force based at Andrews Air Force Base near Washington. If the general's string-pulling worked, it looked like my days of living the dream in the South Pacific just might be coming to an end.

Chapter Ten

Apparently, the general had made some contacts because, before I knew it, I was headed back to the states. However, I was not headed to Andrews and the 89th. First, I had to do some time in Omaha, Nebraska.

At first I thought I was back in a place like South Dakota, just not quite as cold. I had never adapted to the local environment in South Dakota, but I did enjoy Omaha only because of the people. They were friendly. In the Air Force I had learned at least one big life lesson – how to adapt to different kinds of people.

Five of us ended up living in one house located one block from the building housing the famous Mutual of Omaha insurance company.

While the flight attendant work had changed my perspective of the Air Force, it still had not convinced me to become a long-time member of the military. It did change my plans on what I wanted to do when I got out though. Instead of tracking down my promised job on Greek cruise ships, now I had my sights on TWA. The airline had added Boeing 747s to the fleet and they were hiring male flight attendants. That was what I saw in my future, but again, the Air Force was about to lay another prospective change on me. That would happen when I got the call to visit with the 89th.

It was the spring of 1970 when I arrived at Andrews Air Force Base. The moment I saw the nice Boeing 707s lined up on the ramp I made the decision I could do this a little while longer. However, not in my wildest dreams did I consider the "little while longer" would be until 1994.

I was now a member of the famous 89th Wing and quickly discovered I was one of the youngest guys there. This is where the previous experiences of my whole life paid off, from the days pulling wagons on Fire Island for the rich and famous to working at Talisman Yacht Club. I had also learned by working with older crew members and flight attendants at my previous bases. I learned from the mistakes of others. I had matured fast and that helped me fit in with the senior Air Force people who served at Andrews. In fact, a senior NCO stationed there would soon tell me I was a lot more mature than anyone he had met who was my age.

The transition from flying in the KC-97s to the 707s was quite a step up. I was now serving in a plane that actually had windows! Plus, we had the luxury of actual tray carriers and a nice galley. This plane carried five flight attendants on board in addition to a very professional crew.

While I had flown with some big military brass on board on Guam and in Omaha, now I was serving some big political players traveling on the 707s out of Andrews. One of those was Secretary of State William Rogers, who served in that post from 1969 until 1973.

Traveling with Sec. Rogers was a first-class operation. During our trips to the Middle East we would typically leave Washington at a reasonable hour and arrive at our destination around 4:00 in the afternoon, in time for dinner and cocktails. The next day, it would be 2:00 in the afternoon when we were wheels up with our arrival at the next destination in only about an hour. Again, just in time for dinner and cocktails.

When our mission in the Middle East would wrap up we would depart and take a rest stop on the way back in Rome. It was easy work.

One of our Middle Eastern trips stands out strongly in my memories. We were in Jordan where Sec. Rogers was a guest at King Hussein's palace. The protocol was relatively comfortable. Our flight crew sat with Hussein's flight crew.

King Hussein respected pilots because he was an aviator himself. He had a DC-10 and flew helicopters, too.

His flight crew and ours were sitting at a beautiful dinner table. Imagine my surprise when Hussein's flight crew began to speak to us and had better command of the English language than some of us! I found out they all had attended the Harvard School of Business.

At one point, Hussein's chief pilot turned to me and said, "You Americans are an amazing people. You are so many different races, so many nationalities, so many different ethnic groups and so many different religions. You are such a melting pot of people from all over the world, yet you are co-existing peacefully."

They say sixty percent of our communication is non-verbal. Apparently, the look on my face was revealing what I was thinking. At the time I was living in Washington and there was a great deal of social unrest in the country, more than I had ever seen in my life. There were anti-war demonstrations and racial conflicts. Many turned violent. It was definitely a turbulent time. So, I must have been projecting my thought, "How can he think we are co-existing peacefully?"

Without me saying a word, he picked up on what was going through my mind.

"I know what you are thinking," he said. "You have unrest in your country, but you're not killing each other. We in the Arab world are of the same race, the same religion and same ethnic group. Yet, our prejudice between our different tribes is stronger than you will ever imagine. Right now, if Saudi Arabia needed a special, technically-gifted person to save their country and the only one available was Jordanian, they wouldn't hire him.

"We've been killing each other for thousands of years," he went on. "Our hatred is so deep and so passionate. That's why I admire you Americans."

I'll never forget his remarks as long as I live and I especially think about what he said in context to what is happening in the world right now. His statement, made over 40 years ago, about the state of the Middle East, is just as pertinent today.

The days serving Secretary Rogers were predictable and easy, especially when you compare them to what was waiting for us around the bend. In September of 1973 a new Secretary of State took the helm. He had been serving as a National Security Advisor to the President since 1969. This man was about to change the face of history and our work schedule substantially. I was about to be hopping continents like never before and working harder and longer hours than I ever had. Our new boss was now a man named Dr. Henry Kissinger.

Chapter Eleven

Within a few months of taking office, Sec. Kissinger found himself in a world where hostilities were peaking in the Middle East following the Yom Kippur War. His back-and-forth trips to the region, in an attempt to bring some peace, became so frequent and so well-known that a new term was coined for his work – shuttle diplomacy.

Several non-commissioned officers served as stewards on Kissinger's shuttle diplomacy missions. Three of them included Carl Resnick, Denny Huelsbeck and me. One of us would be in charge of running the mission.

Unlike the iron-clad, predictable itineraries of Sec. Rogers, now we would receive an itinerary simply worded, "Andrews to London as directed." The "as directed" part was one we would quickly learn could mean absolutely anything and totally unpredictable.

The problem was in trying to plan for a mission you had no idea would be for how long and to where. Since we had to provide all the food and beverages for Dr. Kissinger and his staff for the entire trip, it became practically impossible to have any definite plans. So, with no specifics, I would simply go down to the State Department, explain our dilemma and sign out $10,000 in cash. Remember, we would be in all kinds of countries. So, writing a check would not be an option in some of them and credit cards were not as prevalent, especially around the world, as they are today.

When Dr. Kissinger was on board our 707, headed east, it was always an adventure into the unknown. We would perhaps end up in London as our first stop and then leave the next day for Moscow. We may be in Moscow for 18 hours and then get word we were headed to Israel. The next day we could end up in Aswan and fly off to Damascus the following day.

It was constantly like that. This is where being the younger guy on the crew paid off. I guess I could take it better than some others.

One trip was especially grueling and one I'll never forget. This trip also revealed a great deal about how Dr. Kissinger was successful in working major deals between countries with totally opposite goals. On this trip he was putting together a peace initiative with Syria. We were wheels up out of Andrews Air Force Base believing we were headed for a 16-day mission to the Middle East. When all was said and done, after shuttling all over the area, we had been working straight and overseas for 34 days; and it was 34 days of being ready to go at any moment.

Thirty days into the mission we had only had rare, partial days off. On one of those days we were called back to duty so we could make an unplanned trip to Damascus. We had no idea if we would be in Damascus for eight hours or eighteen hours. Our orders were to be ready to go within an hour's notice, every hour on the hour.

After experiencing Dr. Kissinger at work, up close and personal, I began to see how he worked. He used anything and everything he could to reach his goals, and that included the airplane.

The reason we would just sit at the airport waiting for him was because the airplane and its crew were being used not just to shuttle the Secretary of State and his staff around, but also as a system to send classified information back to Washington. We didn't believe Kissinger trusted the local embassies with the information, so he would use the airplane's communication system and radio operators for that part of the mission.

On flights with the previous Secretary of State, we would normally have two radio operators on board. With Kissinger there were two radio operators plus two crypto-maintenance guys on the flight. They would stay on board the plane and work the entire time. This was in the pre-digital communication days, so they were operating large Telex-type machines. While we sat on the ramp, frequently there would be vans loading classified information into the plane for transmission to Washington.

On some rare occasions we would get the chance to actually go stay in a hotel when on these missions, but that wasn't without risk. Originally, on these trips, the crew commuted by bus to Jerusalem. However, while we were on one mission, Jerusalem was the victim of a rocket attack. After that we would base out of Tel Aviv. It was a long drive between Tel Aviv and Jerusalem making the trips even more exhausting.

Some of the classiest members of the press I worked with in my days as an Air Force flight attendant were those traveling with us during these Kissinger shuttle diplomacy days. On board we had reporters like Marvin Kalb of CBS, Richard Valeriani of NBC, Ted Koppel of ABC and several others. It seemed to us they were a classier group of reporters than were assigned to cover the White House at that time. Kissinger knew how to use the information he shared with these reporters to his benefit, too.

When we arrived in Israel from Damascus, the press was waiting for the latest from Dr. Kissinger. He reported, "The talks have broken down. I'm going back to Washington tomorrow since there is nothing I can do right now."

The next morning all of the passengers and bags were loaded on the plane. But, instead of heading to Washington, as Kissinger had told the press, he told us, "We have to go back to Damascus to say goodbye."

While we were in the air, newspapers around the world were reporting what he had told the press, the peace talks had failed. I was starting to see how Kissinger worked. He knew very well that to Arabs negotiation was one of their favorite sports. He had played the press and, apparently, the Arabs loved it.

Finally, after 34 grueling days, there was a peace initiative with Syria.

While the game of negotiations may have been successful for the world, it wasn't necessarily scoring points with the wives. Kissinger's wife, Nancy, who he met when she worked for David Rockefeller, was on that grueling trip and she was worn out like the rest of us.

"When are we going home?" she was heard asking Kissinger at some point into the mission.

"Never, never, never," he responded.

My wife had been trying to gauge when I might be returning to the states by watching the news. She was watching the CBS Evening News with Walter Cronkite the night Marvin Kalb reported that the peace talks had broken down and we were headed back to Washington. It didn't happen.

"Tell Marvin Kalb I'll never believe another word Walter Cronkite says," she told me on the phone when I had to break the news that we would not be headed back after all.

A lot of our travel with Dr. Kissinger was classified. Everyone who worked for Kissinger, traveling in the Middle East and during the end of the Viet Nam war, believed his philosophy in the Middle East was to keep everybody equally powerful. I don't think he saw an end to the problems there. We knew we were making history on these trips. It was an intense, educational and magnificent time for our country.

Chapter Twelve

There was one mission involving Dr. Kissinger I was not on but certainly heard about via fellow flight attendant, Bernie Palmer. After hearing the story, I was thankful I was not on that trip.

The plane dropped Kissinger off in France and then repositioned in Germany and waited for him. When his business was finished on this trip, the plane was brought to Paris. As Dr. Kissinger was walking to the plane news broke that the Americans had accidently bombed the French embassy in Viet Nam. As a result, before he could board, he was called back to Paris for talks. The plane and the crew just sat there on the ramp in Paris and waited. For 56 hours they waited.

Just in case Kissinger finished up and was ready to go, they had a system arranged where they had French air traffic control releases for departure every hour on the hour. As the hours passed, they ran out of food on the plane. The captain did not know if he should cater a meal or not, knowing they might leave any moment. Finally, the captain had some food brought out to the plane.

The crew chief told me that before the food was finally catered after almost 56 hours, the last meal he remembered having was white bread with canned gravy on it. I'm sure that catered meal was a welcome event.

When all was said and done, and we had finally returned to the good, 'ole USA, the mission could have been called a success. However, it had taken a toll on a lot of the crew. As a result of that one trip, five of them retired from the Air Force. It was even the last mission for the chief steward of the 89th at that time, Doyle Whitehead. That's how tough that trip was.

For quite a while after the Kissinger shuttle diplomacy days were over, Barry Schweid and I would run into each other now and then. One of us would always ask, "Have you been to Jerusalem?"

The other would respond, "Have I been to Jerusalem?"

While we all were wiped out during and after that 34-day trip, it always amazed us that Kissinger seemed to have endless energy. During the mission, the press asked him how he was holding up, considering his staff, the press and the crew were totally exhausted.

"When you're on the high wire and your winning, you have energy," Kissinger said.

A long-time friend, Frank Rice, who served in the Air Force as a crew chief, put Kissinger's energy in understandable terms when I visited with him in Florida after I retired from the military. He ran a very successful tow truck business, bringing in a million dollars a year when that was big money.

Despite his enormous success, he often worked twelve hours a day, seven days a week. During my visit we were out on his 38-foot Hatteras. We were cruising and relaxing on a Sunday afternoon, yet he was doing business on the phone. When he hung up I asked him about his hard work.

"Frank, how do you do it?" I asked him. "I'm impressed with your lifestyle and with the money you're making, but I'm not impressed with the hours you're putting into it."

He answered my question with two questions for me.

"Howie, have you ever played Monopoly late at night with a bunch of people?" he said. "Were you more tired when you were winning or when you were losing?"

Frank had put things in perspective and I immediately thought of Kissinger. He was winning and that fueled him.

Since the days of working on the shuttle diplomacy missions I've been frequently asked what I personally thought of Dr. Kissinger. I can say he obviously subscribed to what was a different management style than we have today. The current trend of stroking employees and being lavish with praise was not common then.

So, he came up in the days when there was a little fear and intimidation used. If he ever said, "You did good," it really meant something coming from him.

As long as you were honest with him, he could handle it, even if you messed up. But, if you started giving him bologna he would not put up with it.

Once, I had misread some schedule information and woke some people up I wasn't supposed to. When Kissinger got wind, he was angry.

"Who did that!" he said.

"I did," I confessed.

Fessing up was obviously the right thing to do because it seemed to immediately cool Kissinger. He simply responded, "Okay."

I feel really fortunate to have been given what I think is one of the biggest compliments he paid to anybody during his days as Secretary of State and, perhaps, during my entire time in the Air Force. One day he turned to me and said, "You treat me better than an old Jewish mother."

Chapter Thirteen

The shuttle diplomacy missions were tough on the entire crew. In addition to the instability of a fixed schedule I was challenged with trying to keep variety in the menu of food served on board during the mission.

Since usual trips had a more fixed schedule, I usually had about eight basic menus I would draw from for a trip. This time, though, with no idea when we would return, I had to get creative to keep from getting repetitious. In fact, before the monster, 34-day trip, I had actually made a visit to a McDonald's in Washington. I was able to commandeer a collection of the famous McDonald's serving paraphernalia, including cups, hats, wrappers and even their tray liners. Even though we prepared all the food on the plane, we wrapped some sandwiches in McDonald's wrappers and used their cups to mix things up a bit. That became a big hit while we were in the Middle East.

In fact, I have a photo in my office taken of Henry Kissinger during a mission. He is wearing a McDonald's hat. As the photo was being taken, Kissinger looked into the camera and said, "What am I, the manager?"

I've been told I am not the only one who has a copy of that photo hanging in his office. Apparently, the chairman of the board of McDonald's does, too.

Trying to keep everyone happy with food during these Middle East missions did cause a few people to dislike us flight attendants. They worked in the local embassies. Since we were not local experts on where to buy food there, we would drop into the local embassies and, on some occasions, clear out their pantries. That didn't put us on their friends list.

Even raiding the local embassy food pantry didn't always meet our needs. Once, trying to add some kind of variety to what we were eating, I mixed together some canned fruit cocktail and canned grapes, adding some cream and cinnamon. Kissinger took one look at it and said, "What the hell is that shit?"

"It's fruit salad," I said. "It's good, try it."

He tried it and he ate it.

One story circulated for years involving Dr. Kissinger. The story is officially nowhere to be found in the world of the Secret Service. They are brothers of the badge and, as the story goes, would not document it.

Until Kissinger's high-profile, potentially dangerous missions, the Secretary of State used State Department security personnel. In Kissinger's case, he was assigned Secret Service protection. After all, in some parts of the Middle East, he was a wanted man.

According to the story the only thing Kissinger wanted from the Secret Service agents was for them to be his body guard. Nothing else. In fact, I was told a story that he would frequently give a test to new agents assigned to his detail.

Kissinger carried a large number of what we called "navigator bags," hard cases he kept important, secure documents in. When a new agent would arrive he would say, "Take my bags." If the agent picked up a bag, he was fired. He definitely did not want his security distracted by anything other than threats to his wellbeing. He expected the agent to reply, "I'm not your bag man, I'm your bodyguard."

It became obvious long after the shuttle diplomacy missions ended that what Kissinger may have lacked in giving compliments to his staff and crew, he made up for it in loyalty. Many who worked for him became very high-level officials. He obviously put a team together of quality people who knew what they were doing.

Many people who served under Dr. Kissinger during the shuttle diplomacy missions and the end of the Viet Nam war went on to become high-ranking officials in government working in foreign affairs.

While Kissinger may not have been a touchy-feely type of boss, he certainly was not alone. As in any work, you hear stories about leaders who colleagues had worked for in the past. Based on those stories, Kissinger was much easier to work for than a former president, Lyndon B. Johnson.

Stories were well shared in the Air Force that President Johnson had fired one of his flight attendants several times. One Air Force One pilot was promoted to general by Johnson. He was Gen. Walter Kross.

Not long ago, Gen. Kross told me a story about his days serving Johnson.

"You know President Johnson promoted me to general, but he still always called me 'Major'," he said.

Obviously, Johnson ruled by a bit of intimidation.

During the Johnson administration there was a smaller group of personnel serving on Air Force One than there is today. He would occasionally call Gen. Kross and say, "We've got to plan this trip, but don't tell anybody."

Sensing Gen. Kross' silence, Johnson knew what he was thinking. "How am I supposed to pull this off without telling anybody?"

Johnson obviously believed that his style and some of his decisions in domestic policy were not very popular.

"I'm not going to have a friend in the world," Johnson is quoted as having once said.

Chapter Fourteen

Henry Kissinger is best known for his work during the shuttle diplomacy missions, but he was also front and center during another major crisis affecting the world at that time – the Viet Nam War, the same war that inspired me to make the choice to sign-up for the Air Force in the first place.

Kissinger was also making frequent trips to China and Russia to discuss issues with them as well. There were tense times all over the globe. But, my days as a flight attendant for him were coming to an end.

While on a trip to South America with Dr. Kissinger, I got a phone call from Charlie Palmer, the chief steward of Air Force One. He wanted to see me. It was in April of 1976, America's bicentennial year.

Charlie offered me a crack at serving on the president's plane.

"We can't guarantee you a job. Anything can happen," Charlie told me. "President Ford has just six months left and they could replace the whole crew then."

Next thing you know, this guy from Long Island, New York, who had originally had no intentions to stay in the Air Force beyond a few years, was now walking up the steps to report to duty on board Air Force One.

It was not a difficult transition for me since I had served as a flight attendant for then Vice-President Gerald Ford during the Nixon years. Now, I would be working for him in his role as president.

In fact, Ford was not the only vice-president I had served on official flights. I had worked under Spiro Agnew, who was Richard Nixon's Vice-President, and I would work with Nelson Rockefeller during his days as Vice-President during the Ford administration.

I found Vice-President Agnew to be a class act. We always traveled on reasonable schedules with him.

I had worked on missions that took him all over the country and the world. He really liked Maryland Crab Salad.

Air Force Two, the call sign given the plane carrying the vice president, had a small crew, usually three flight attendants. They would bring over extra crew to augment that on some missions and I was one of those. Basically, I was running a mission in the background that the rest of the stewards were responsible for.

Once, during a flight to Europe, I went to a deli and bought a can of frozen crab. Back at the plane I was defrosting it when the chief steward of Air Force Two noticed what I was doing.

"What are you doing?" he asked me.

"Sir, I'm going to make him his crab salad that you ordered."

He looked surprised and said, "Don't you know he never eats frozen crab!"

"He's been eating it for five days," I said.

I guess he never noticed the difference.

Agnew's biggest battles during his days as second-in-command seemed to be with the press. He was so frustrated at being misquoted in the media that he literally carried his own stenographer on trips. When he was questioned by the press about something he supposedly said he was prepared.

"Wait a minute, that's not what I said," Agnew would say, challenging a reporter. "Here's what I said."

He would then read his quote taken by the stenographer.

I happened to be working on Vice-President Agnew's last official flight. He was speaking in Chicago and the crew was in a room watching him on television. When we landed back in D.C., we saw them taking the furniture out of the Air Force Two office he worked in. We knew that wasn't a good sign. We did not know that would be his last flight.

During Vice President Rockefeller's days I remembered that his wife, Happy, had been a regular at the Talisman Yacht Club on Fire Island during my youthful days working there.

Despite the years since I had seen her, she walked aboard Air Force Two and said, "Howie!"

I responded with, "Rose Mateus!" It was her wine of choice during her visits to the Talisman.

Seeing her gave me a flashback to my days working at the yacht club. Word had got out that Rockefeller was going to be visiting. This was before he was married to Happy. He was going through a divorce during a time when divorce was a dirty word. He heard that a reporter might be at the Talisman Yacht Club and knew he would be questioned about his marriage. So, he didn't show up.

In retrospect, President Ford was the only President I worked for that did not have the ego of an elected President, because he was not elected. He was cast into the office upon the resignation of Richard Nixon.

From my perspective, Ford took his job seriously. He certainly wasn't new to public service, considering he had been a long-time member of Congress. He saw himself as an employee of the people of the United States.

Anytime a president is in office comedians and impersonators lie in wait looking for some quirk or mannerism they can use to imitate or tease the president about. For President Ford it was a few tumbles he took coming down the steps of Air Force One that would be used on even *Saturday Night Live* to mock him.

From a few small slips on the steps to practically falling down, most of them in Salzburg, Austria, they were all caught on tape and used all over the media.

Despite these mishaps, Ford was a great athlete. He was not the klutz they tried to make him out to be. In fact, look closely at the incident in Austria and you'll see that only a real athlete could make a recovery like that. In reality, Ford was a great snow skier and a former football player. Both he and his wife, Betty, were homespun Michigan folks who were a pleasure to work for.

I'll never forget a running joke President Ford had going with me. Since he was on Air Force One before I was stationed on board, he would frequently say, "Howie, remember, I got here first."

Ford never walked onto Air Force One without stopping where the Presidential Pilot, Col. McClellan, and the crew were waiting. He would say, "How are the boys doing?"

When I became part of the Air Force One team Ford was trying to become the nominee for the Republican presidential ticket. The party was splintered into different factions and he was trying diligently to try and bring them back together.

He was obviously reflective during the campaign. Once, during a stop, he boarded Air

Force One and came into the State Room. It was just him and me.

"You know, Howie, there's only one way you can conquer your enemy," President Ford said.

"How is that, sir?" I asked.

"If you fight your enemy, kill your enemy, the war continues. It never stops. But, if you can make your enemy your friend, you've conquered."

The time serving Ford would be a brief one. Just six short months after walking onto the plane as an Air Force flight attendant serving the president there was an election. A peanut farmer from Plains, Georgia was going to be moving into the White House and we all wondered if we were about to be moved off of the plane. After all, it had been common for a new administration in the White House to result in all kinds of staff changes.

Chapter Fifteen

Working on any presidential detail could be compared with working for a large corporation that is being sold. You expect the new owners to make changes to the staff. Rumors were running through the 89th that when Jimmy Carter took the Oath of Office changes would be made to the Air Force One crew. Fortunately, that didn't happen.

It was quite an experience for me transitioning to a large group of people on board who were primarily from the South. It's not that I had never worked with such genteel people from below the Mason-Dixon Line before.

There were some southern people I had served in the past, just not such a large group. Prior to President Carter, I had flown with a Congressman from Charleston, South Carolina named Mendel Rivers. I learned quickly that if you had Congressman Rivers on a flight you better have grits on board or you were in trouble.

On one flight, Rivers was in the plane's state room speaking with fellow Congressmen about a trip they were making to a military base. He was giving his colleagues some advice.

"Now listen, when you talk to people down there, don't ask the generals anything, ask the sergeants," he said. "The generals may lie to you. The sergeants tell you the truth."

I quickly learned that southern people could be matter of fact. The members of the Carter administration were going to prove that.

We were now flying him and his staff, and they generally were nice people. However, we found out that one particular member of his staff didn't care much for us and he showed it. He was Jody Powell, Carter's press secretary.

There was a protocol regarding meals served on Air Force One. Anyone who ate a meal on board was charged for it. Prior to Carter's administration, bills for food and drinks served to president's staff and guests would be sent to the White House for payment. New rules from the new president stated that we would now present everyone with a bill at the end of the day for what they had consumed during the day's flights. They would have to sign off on the bill before it was sent to the White House to be paid. If it was a staff member, the bill would be applied against their per diem. For some reason, Powell didn't like the system at all.

When I took his bill to him to be signed he wrinkled it up and threw it at me. No one else in the Carter administration treated us that way.

I guess I had to think about my Coke bottles back at Lackland Air Force Base during days like that. I always had those Coke bottles in the back of my mind.

I also wasn't alone in being uncomfortable with the way Jody Powell addressed the new President the first month we had him on Air Force One. He called Carter "Jimbo" all the time. Many of us felt this was disrespectful to the office and apparently we were not by ourselves. Soon, he stopped doing that and called him "Mr. President."

A lady Air Force One crew member, who would later become my wife, experienced an uncomfortable encounter with Jody Powell when he started talking to famous Associated Press reporter Helen Thomas about the mating habits of farm animals using vulgar language.

Powell's antics naturally created some friction between him and the crew because we had to deal with him on a personal level.

Powell also dealt with the media a lot differently than other press secretaries. Once, Powell came to the back of the plane and shouted at Sam Donaldson, the ABC News reporter known for being tough.

"Hey, Sam, I've got a flash for you," Powell said. "President Carter just called Reagan an (expletive deleted)!"

Sam Donaldson fired back, "How am I supposed to report that? 'President Carter said (expletive deleted)?'"

Believe it or not, soft drinks are a big deal on Air Force One. Incredibly, every time a different political party takes over the White House, a different brand of soda ends up on board. It's all about politics.

In the past, Coca-Cola was known to be a big supporter of the Democrats, while Pepsi donated big to the Republicans. So, when Carter came aboard, Pepsis were gone and Coke became the soft drink of choice.

To a few on the Carter team, even trying to serve them a soft drink was problematic. We had to charge a dollar for a drink. Some members of the Carter staff would bring a bottle of booze on board and order a Coke for their set up.

"I suppose you're going to charge me for the Coke?" some would ask.

"Somebody has to pay for it," we'd say.

They were obviously upset about it. They also were not happy campers when President Carter had cigarettes, normally donated by the tobacco companies, removed from Air Force One. Jody Powell smoked and he made it clear he didn't like it.

Another difference between Carter's administration and what we had been accustomed to previously was how the White House scheduled trips. At times we felt whoever was planning the missions had no concept of time zones. While the Kissinger missions may have been long periods away from home, the trips involving the Carter years never seemed to sync up with our body clocks. For example, we would have a mission to India and be going to work at what was 6:00 p.m. for our local time. This put us on what was, for us, an all-night flight only to have to return back to the states shortly after arriving. The flight fatigue on some missions was incredible.

Despite the challenges of this new administration on board, our missions were not without some very memorable moments. It was especially interesting when we had President Carter's mother, Lillian, on our flights. She was a genuine character.

Once, Lillian Carter was leading a delegation from the United States to the funeral of the former, well-known Israeli Prime Minister Golda Meir. Our flight plan took us to Madrid for a refueling stop and then into Israel.

One of the challenges of my work was to time out the meals so the passengers would not be eating while we were taking off and landing. It was a safety issue.

As we were approaching Madrid, I was having a little trouble trying to get Miss Lillian to agree it was time to feed everyone in order to time out our fuel stop. In a diplomatic way of trying to push the issue a bit I said, "We could serve this meal and feed you at any time you'd like."

She turned to me and said, "When I eat, they eat." She wasn't brash or rude, just matter of fact.

On the flight between Madrid and Israel it was getting late. Many of the passengers, now fed and comfortable, were asleep. I was taking advantage of the moment to catch a break in the back of the 707. Next thing I know Lillian Carter walks into the area and sits in the jump seat.

She begins to tell me how she is still in awe of her son being President of the United States. She was an obviously proud mother. Then, she surprised me by comparing her two sons.

"You know, it's awful funny, because when the two boys were growing up Jimmy had to work a lot harder to get the same grades that Billy got," she said.

Her statement would have been a big shock to the nation because the President's brother, Billy, had been portrayed in the media as a country bumpkin. He even went on to have a brand of beer named after him. The fact is, Billy was playing the press. In reality, he was a pretty smart guy and very well read.[1]

Throughout the flight, to Israel and back, Lillian Carter spent some of her time playing cards with the passengers. She played cards with the senators in the front of the plane and took their money. She then proceeded to win some funds from a few Secret Service agents in the back of the plane.

---

[1] The co-author of this book met and interviewed Billy Carter in Nashville in the late 1970s. He found Billy Carter extremely intelligent, articulate and a voracious reader.

On another trip, Miss Lillian, as she was affectionately called, decided her slip was too long. She asked me for a pair of scissors. She cut her slip and gave the excess to a senator who was on the flight.

Lillian Carter was fantastic and, as they would say down south, it was a hoot to have her on board.

The other Mrs. Carter I had the pleasure of serving was the President's wife, Rosalynn. She is the epitome of a genuine southern lady.

Chapter Sixteen

Near the end of Carter's time in office, a period during a president's term when they are normally out seeking re-election, he was not spending much time on the campaign trail. Terrorists in Iran were holding many Americans hostage at the American Embassy in Tehran. As a result, President Carter felt it was more important to stay in Washington and attempt to find a way to bring the hostage crisis to an end.

As a result, his wife made many campaign appearances on his behalf.

When the First Lady is on board, without the President, the plane she is traveling in is not referred to as Air Force One. That is a call sign reserved only for any airplane the President is on board. So, Mrs. Carter made many trips on a DC-9.

Another Air Force One flight attendant, Denny Stump, and I were assigned to run the missions the first lady traveled on during her husband's campaign. Denny and I had an arrangement where he would run one mission and I would run the next. It was imperative that we communicated from time to time in order to make sure we all were singing off the same hymn sheet on these flights.

Once, during a few hectic days, I lost track of Denny. The White House communications staff is incredible. They seem to have a way to track down anybody.

I had an upcoming mission to work on the first lady's plane and needed to speak with Denny about what he had served on her current flight and other details. He was in Chicago on the ground. These were the days before cell phones. So, I called the communications guys at the White House and asked them to please find Denny.

On the mission he was working Air Force One was on the ground and the first lady had flown up in her separate, executive plane. Denny was on the ramp near her DC-9 when the red light on the beige phone near the base of Air Force One, which is always there as a security contact for the President or his staff when the plane is on the ground, began to flash. Naturally, it got everyone's attention.

The pilot on the first lady's plane was standing next to Denny and said, "Wow, wonder what that's about."

Since the president and his staff had already left the plane area Denny walked over and answered the phone. He spoke on it for a while and then made his way back to the first lady's plane.

"What is going on?" several crew members asked.

"It was for me," Denny said.

It really was. On the other end of the line was me. The White House communications gurus had worked their magic and had tracked down Denny just for me. I'm sure some of his fellow crew members still wonder who was on the line and why Denny, a master sergeant flight attendant, was being called on the President's special phone.

During President Carter's final year in office, I was working with the first lady. She was on a trip to campaign on behalf of her husband. It was February and we were headed to Maine. We were informed the temperature where we were headed was 26 degrees below zero.

Mrs. Carter had a very heavy coat on board that I believe was made in Afghanistan. It was lined with fleece on the inside and, after a few more layers, was suede on the outside. It probably weighed ten pounds.

After we landed and had taxied up to our parking spot the steps were rolled up to the plane. I grabbed Mrs. Carter's heavy coat and held it up behind her so she could slide her arms through the sleeves and I would lift it on to her shoulders. At least that was the plan.

As I held the heavy coat for this genteel southern lady, she quickly slid her arms down the sleeves. However, one of her hands exited a sleeve and struck me right in the groin. It was a direct hit.

She was incredibly embarrassed and I was, too. We just looked at each other with an uncomfortable grin while each of us blushed a little.

We returned to Washington that night and when I arrived home I told my wife the story.

"Well, that was a touching experience," she said.

Two days after that event Mrs. Carter was back on the campaign trail for the president, while he still remained in Washington dealing with the Iranian hostage crisis. The destination was again, Maine. I had no intentions of even insinuating the "touching experience" had even happened. After all, I looked at my job like playing golf. If you hit a bad ball one day you didn't think about it the next time you had to tee up. I was focusing on this flight, this mission, not what happened two days ago no matter how embarrassing it was for both of us.

When we landed at the first stop, I gathered Mrs. Carter's coat. As I approached her from behind to help with her coat she turned towards me and gently said, "Howie."

"Yes, ma'am," I said.

"Do you notice I now have a caped coat?"

Sure enough, she had changed coats and now had a caped one on board. How brilliant is that? She was probably concerned that she could repeat the event from two days ago, even with someone other than me.

I would see Mrs. Carter aboard Air Force One again during a trip to carry a delegation, including her husband, to the funeral of Anwar Sadat, the assassinated leader of Egypt.

We were returning to the United States from the funeral late at night. At one point, Mrs. Carter came to the area on the plane where I was working and sat down on a jump seat. She spent about 45 minutes with me reflecting on her husband's days as president.

"Howie, he was always so concerned about losing his bag," she said. "You guys never lost his bag. But, the first trip we took after he left office, they lost his bag."

Mrs. Carter said she missed us and the days of her flights on the plane.

Rosalynn Carter was a delightful lady to be around. Plus, I don't know how many people realize how intelligent she is. She worked very hard and I know she was personally involved in writing all of her own speeches. She was also fluent in Spanish, so if she had to give a speech to a predominantly Spanish-speaking audience, she was involved in writing those, too.

She was a warm, comfortable and professional first lady.

In reality, I worked more for Mrs. Carter than for her husband. Charlie Palmer, the man who hired me aboard the president's plane was the Chief Steward on Air Force One at the time. As a result, Charlie worked the front of the plane and had the most interaction with President Carter.

Based on the times I did interact with President Carter, I would describe him as almost like a professor. He seemed to enjoy sharing knowledge with people. To this day, many people do not know that Carter had studied engineering at the Georgia Institute of Technology and at the Naval Academy. While in the Navy, he worked on a nuclear submarine program with Admiral Hyman Rickover.

Charlie Palmer, the Chief Steward, was also from Georgia and, therefore, certainly spoke the President's language.

Chapter Seventeen

One of the advantages of serving aboard the president's plane was that you became privy to some interesting stories about things that happened when the president was not on board. One of my favorites about Carter was shared by two Secret Service agents who were aboard the back-up plane, where I was assigned, during a flight to Japan. The agents said the event happened just a few days prior to the flight we were on.

Apparently, during a trip back home to Plains, President Carter decided he wanted to go fishing. He had invited his doctor, Dr. Lukash, and military aide Col. Peterson. So, in the heat of a Georgia summer, when it is 95 degrees in the morning, they made their way, along with the president's security detail, to a tiny pond within a forest of pine trees. Anyone familiar with these southern ponds knows they are frequently filled with large lily pads and slime, while the air around them is filled with hungry mosquitoes.

After a period of no luck catching a fish, President Carter turned to his guests and said, "Let's go swimming." While his guests must have thought he had to be kidding, he wasn't. Carter jumped into the pond.

When he asked Col. Peterson to join him, the colonel said, "Oh, no, I can't do that, sir, because I have the football."

The football is the security briefcase that accompanies the President wherever he goes. The irony of Col. Peterson quickly using it as an excuse not to jump into the pond did not go unnoticed by the Secret Service agents. The colonel had a reputation of not making any decisions quickly. So, that fact made the story even more entertaining.

"He made the first quick decision of his whole career," the agent telling the story said.

The Secret Service agent also found himself in an unusual situation when it came to his duty in protecting the President of the United States.

"You know, we were standing there and he's swimming in this pond. God knows what is in that pond. How would we write that one up? 'The president got eaten in a pond?'"

President Carter's trips down south also affected the usual attire of Secret Service agents assigned to him. They normally liked to dress well. Nice suits and Gucci shoes is what they usually wore. But after a trip to Jekyll Island with the President to a little cottage there, they looked entirely different the next time we headed there. Fatigue pants, snake boots and snake sticks had replaced the suits.

"There were more critters down there than we've ever seen in our life," one of the agents said.

Although we were Air Force One flight attendants, it was not unusual to work on other flights with passengers other than the president. Once I was on a flight taking Vice-President Walter Mondale on a routine trip. A DC-9 was the plane acting as Air Force Two on that trip.

With the exception of a state room at the front of the plane, this version of the DC-9 was mostly cattle call seating like you would find on an airline. There was a small desk area with a typewriter on it in the back of the plane.

During this flight a high-ranking military aide on the plane needed something typed. That's when it was discovered the typewriter was, in aviation lingo, in-op, or, in civilian terms, it was not working.

Using the phone system on the plane, the aide called the vice-chief's office at the Pentagon.

"What's wrong with the typewriter on this airplane?" he asked them.

That question set off a series of events that could only happen in a government operation.

The Pentagon called the 89th Wing at Andrews Air Force Base where we were based. They, of course, had no idea what was wrong with the typewriter in the back of the DC-9. So, what did they do? They bridged the call right back to the plane and to the flight deck and the captain on board. This meant the military aide in the back of the plane, sitting at the dead typewriter, was now on the phone with the captain on the flight deck in the front of the plane via a call that had been routed from the plane to the Pentagon to Andrews Air Force Base and back to the plane.

Needless to say, this did nothing to fix the typewriter.

The Carter years went by quickly. He lost the election which meant we were, again, facing the possibility of a crew change on the president's plane. The new commander in chief was going to be the former governor of California and an actor.

· Chapter Eighteen

While we were never sure if a crew change on Air Force One would take place when a new resident moved into the White House, apparently the consistency during the change from the Ford to the Carter administration had not gone unnoticed. Perhaps the powers that be realized that having a steady, seasoned crew on the most recognized plane on the planet, carrying the leader of the free world, was a good thing.

With the occasional conflict between a few members of President Carter's staff, we were wondering what the atmosphere of the new administration would be. I was curious about the man who had just been elected, Ronald Reagan.

I had worked for a lot of politicians at this point. I worked for Ted Kennedy when he had brown hair. So, being around these elected officials, I had learned that what you see is not always what you get. Sometimes politicians are not what you see on camera.

We did hear some feedback about the man who would soon be in the White House from the press. We were traveling with President Carter on a trip to Phoenix, Arizona. Ronald Reagan had been elected, but had not yet been sworn into office. He was in Phoenix, too, and the press went to see him.

When the press returned to the plane, most of them were laughing.

"What's so funny?" I asked them.

"This guy's funny," one of them answered, referring to Reagan.

During Carter's presidency, he had made news after a Playboy interview with him. He was asked about sex in the interview and he responded that he had lusted before in his heart. Carter was confessing and being honest. So, when the media ran into Reagan, they decided to ask him about sex, too.

"We asked him, 'Gov. Reagan, four years ago, when Carter took office, he was asked what his thoughts on sex were. We'd like to hear your comments on the subject."

Reagan was 69 years old. The member of the press telling me the story said the president-elect responded with, "At 2:00 o'clock in the afternoon, after a warm shower, I think it's wonderful."

The basics about the new president I knew. He was an actor. He had been the governor of California and had a good record in that job. But, being honest now, I didn't know what we were going to get. I think I was on guard to see if we could catch him being a phony. It wouldn't take long for me to have that question answered.

The first time I worked on a flight with him, he had been elected but had not been sworn in. We were in a DC-9 in California to pick him up. It was the same time period John Lennon had been shot. He was very gracious on the plane.

When we picked him up in California to bring him to Washington to take office, I was given a tip that the flight attendants on board would heed during his eight years as president.

As some of his staff was boarding the airplane, I recognized a man I had served before. He was a former member of Nelson Rockefeller's staff and we spoke in the back of the plane.

"Howie, you got a birthday cake on this airplane?" he asked.

"Well, no, sir," I said. "I don't think so."

"I want to give you a heads up. This man likes celebrating birthdays. I don't care if it's a crew member or a staff member, no matter who is on that plane, he likes birthdays."

That tip ended up being an important one. The entire time he was president, the chief flight attendant at the time, Charlie Palmer, saw to it we kept a cake on board Air Force One, just in case. It didn't matter if it was a security person, a member of the maintenance crew, a pilot, a staff member, or a congressman; if President Reagan found out it was your birthday, out came a cake.

There was one incident that did leave us with a little egg on our face over a birthday cake. Just before leaving on a trip to the take the President out to California, we got word it was Jerry Parr's birthday. He was a Secret Service agent who happened to be heading up the security detail when Reagan was shot by John Hinckley, Jr. in a demented attempt to catch the attention of actress Jodi Foster.

Chief Steward Charlie Palmer ordered a chocolate cake from the Watergate Bakery. They had a reputation for great cakes.

The problem with this one cake was that it was topped with shaved chocolate. So, here we are in the Secret Service room on Air Force One with Agent Parr, the president and a few others standing around. After we all sing "Happy Birthday," Jerry Parr goes to blow out the candles. The shaved chocolate went all over President Reagan.

Thankfully, Reagan's great demeanor kicked in and he just laughed. But, Charlie Palmer turned to me and said, "No more shaved chocolate."

All of these interactions gave me a good glimpse into Reagan's personality. Then, when I began to work more closely with him, any thoughts that I might catch him being phony were quickly eliminated. I don't care if I went in to give him something as insignificant as a glass of water he would stop and say something to raise my self-esteem. Now that's a boss! How would you like to work for a boss who, every time you were around him, made you feel better about yourself? That was the President Reagan I would come to know.

Trust me, if you were to catch any negative side of someone's personality, you would catch it on Air Force One. We would have them on board for long periods of time. We would even have them sleep on board and would have to wake them up. He was always gracious. He was sincere. It took quite a man to be both humble and presidential. I never caught him being phony. Since I would be spending eight years working for him, his graciousness and sincerity would make my life very enjoyable.

It was during the Reagan presidency that the order was placed for a Boeing 747 version of Air Force One. This happened because of timing.

The fact is Richard Nixon wanted a 747. The 747 came out in 1969.

The other plane being considered to take the role of Air Force One was a modified version of the C5A because it could carry the cars on the same plane that carried the president. However, the C5A had earned a reputation of being a high-maintenance machine. So, that idea was scrapped.

The political winds never blew in Nixon's favor on ordering a 747. Presidents Ford and Carter also wanted a 747, but the timing wasn't there for them either.

President Reagan was the one to order the 747 in the early part of his second term in office.

The 747 version of Air Force One actually did not arrive until 1990. That meant the Reagans never had the opportunity to fly on the plane he ordered as president. That's because it took a while to custom build the airplane.

I believe he would have liked to have been the first president to fly in the new plane. In fact, I once overheard him say, "If I knew I was going to win re-election with such good numbers I would have ordered a 747 the first term."

It's not common knowledge that Nancy Reagan did not get to see the inside of the 747 her husband had ordered until after his death. Yet, she had actually played a big role in determining the look of the plane's interior. She had designed the décor of the plane. Her design was obviously a good one since it has survived the test of time and is still in use today.

I once ran into a colonel who worked at the Pentagon and now lives not far from me in Wilmington, North Carolina. He was involved in the design of the presidential 747.

He said he brought his ideas for the interior to the White House. His samples included usual Air Force colors - dark blues, black and gray. Mrs. Reagan looked them over very graciously. Then, she looked at the colonel and said, "That's very nice, but don't you think it should be in a desert motif?"

Needless to say, the interior of Air Force One was created in a desert motif and it has done very well. She did a heck of a job.

While we are on the subject of the 747 that would arrive in the next administration, it's important to point out that Boeing did something unprecedented in designing Air Force One. The air crew was involved in the design of their work space. So, we took advantage of the space we were assigned to on the plane and worked with Boeing engineers to create the galleys and design the layout of how seats were placed. This opportunity to design our workspace helped create a very efficient operation. We could clean the 747 faster than the 707, even though the 747 was a much bigger plane.

Another aspect of the Reagan administration that made our life more enjoyable aboard the president's plane was the schedule. He was a boss that knew he was boss, so we had a reasonable flight schedule. During his entire eight years in office, I don't think we left Washington earlier than 9:30 in the morning.

That was true even on overseas trips. For example, when we took President Reagan to an economic summit in Japan, it wasn't a last-minute, grueling trip. We would first head to California for a day or two. Then, we would head to Honolulu for a day followed by a day in Guam or someplace similar. That way, when we arrived in Japan, he was fresh and ready to do business with other world leaders.

That was quite a change from what we had been accustomed to in the past. It had been typical for us to have a last-minute, thirteen-hour mission overseas that put us on the ground when our body clock was telling us it was 3:00 in the morning. We would have jetlag, the president would have jetlag and his staff was suffering, too.

President Reagan didn't do it that way. We were thankful. In fact, unless there was some significant change, such as a national security issue, we had our schedule about three months in advance. It was an organized, well-oiled machine.

We were also thankful, and lucky, that we were working for a president who had his home in California. Not only did he really like spending time there, but we did, too. During his eight years in office, I would guess we spent over 380 days in the Golden State. We were treated well there.

When Reagan was first elected, I spent most of my time in the back of Air Force One, working more with the press and his staff members. Charlie Palmer, chief steward at the time, John Haigh and others worked more closely with the president at the front of the plane. When Charlie retired, I became John's deputy and began to have more interaction with the president. I quickly learned he had a great sense of humor.

Because of his love for his home state, he would make reference to it when he boarded the plane by comparing California to our destination. For example, if we were headed to Ohio, he would board the plane and say, "You know, we're going in the right direction, but we're not going far enough."

On one scheduled trip to Texas, I was expecting his usual comment about our destination and its direction to California. Instead, I got a taste of the famous Reagan wit.

"You know, I'm going to Texas, they've got me going to a turkey shoot," he said.

"Yes, sir," I said.

"I don't know why they are sending me to Texas for a turkey shoot. I've got enough turkeys in Washington," he quipped.

There were other advantages for the crew of having a president on board who was from California and who had been an actor. Not the least being the places we stayed and the people we saw.

Typically, when holidays arrived during Reagan's presidency, we would be home for Christmas but leave the next day for Palm Springs. A military ID in Palm Springs would get you onto any golf course and into any movie theater. We stayed at the Gene Autry Hotel. The classic Western movie star turned broadcasting mogul lived in the hotel and was often spotted walking around and talking with guests. Gene Autry was also the man who had made "Rudolph the Red Nosed Reindeer" a big hit on the radio.

The hotel he owned brought back many memories from my childhood. Gene Autry's famous horse, Champion, was preserved in the lobby for all to see. And in the bar, you would frequently see many of the old cowboy stars that had appeared in movies with Gene Autry and Roy Rogers. Anybody in my age group would be as impressed as I was at seeing these big film stars that we grew up watching.

On one flight to California, President Reagan was busily working on rewriting a speech into his style of speaking. He was working in the conference room on board with a few staff members on the other end of the room. For some reason, they had become engrossed in a conversation about the possibility of Hollywood making a movie based on the life of Mickey Rooney.

The president seemed oblivious to their discussion as he worked away. Finally, one of the staff members asked a question of the group discussing Rooney.

"Wonder who they would get to play Mickey Rooney?"

Several names began to float around the room until, finally, one of them said, "Why not get Mickey Rooney to play Mickey Rooney."

President Reagan stopped working and looked up.

"No, he's too short," he said.

Everyone loved President Reagan's sense of humor.

Chapter Nineteen

Another difference between the Carter staff and Reagan's was how they dressed. While the Carter team dressed casually on board, Reagan's staff was always formally dressed.

When Charlie Palmer was chief steward, the subject of attire put him in a difficult position between the president and his wife, Nancy Reagan. However, the president saved the day for all involved.

Air Force One was on a flight to Japan and was making a fuel stop in Alaska. On the approach into the 49th state, President Reagan turned to Charlie and said, "Charlie, I'll take my trench coat, my regular trench coat."

Before Charlie could respond, Nancy did.

"No, Charlie, get him the coat with the fur collar."

This puts someone serving the president in a difficult situation. What does he do? Does he honor the president's request or grab the coat his wife wants him to wear? Sensing the situation and sincerely concerned about everybody involved, the president negotiated with his wife.

"Well, you know, I may be overdressed if I wear the coat with the fur collar," Reagan said.

Nancy simply replied, "You're wearing the coat with the fur collar."

The president gave a bit of nonverbal communication and Charlie grabbed the coat with the fur collar.

When the plane came to a stop on the ramp in Alaska, the wheels were chocked and the doors opened, right on time. As the president is walking towards the door to leave, Charlie hands the president his gloves.

President Reagan took the gloves and smiled. Speaking quietly to Charlie, he said, "Well, I'm not wearing my gloves."

Here were two men, both saving face with each other and the first lady. One of them just so happened to be the President of the United States. Class act.

Nancy Reagan's concern over what coat her husband wore was an example of how much they truly loved each other. They were frequently flirting with each other on the plane. He would point towards her and tell us, "Please give my daughter a glass of water." She would laugh.

You could tell their interaction was sincere and not an act put on around us. You could see them truly caring for each other when they were unaware they were being seen.

In fact, Michael Deaver, who served as President Reagan's deputy chief of staff, told a story about an incident he witnessed while he was working for Reagan when he was the governor of California.

Deaver said he was walking into then-Governor Reagan's office as he was wrapping up a telephone call. As he entered, he noticed his boss slowly leaning towards the phone cradle and almost whispering into the phone. Deaver finally realized Reagan was talking to Nancy on the phone and they were playfully trying to be the last one to say "I love you" before they hung up.

Speaking of Michael Deaver, there was a moment on Air Force One when he got the best of my boss, the chief steward, Charlie Palmer.

Charlie was a great, very dedicated, blue-suiter. He was dedicated to the crew and the president. Since everyone had to pay for their meals on Air Force One, Charlie worked hard to find that tough balance between the best quality and a reasonable price.

Sometimes, word would come down that someone would hear the press plane was serving rack of lamb while we were serving chopped sirloin. There was, of course, a good reason for that.

However, Charlie was called down to the White House where he was informed that Deputy Chief of Staff Deaver wanted to upgrade the meals on Air Force One.

After that meeting, the next meal we served on board was Lobster Thermidor, which is similar to Lobster Newberg with thick chunks of lobster poured back into a lobster shell. It was being served as the dinner meal on a flight from Canada back to Andrews Air Force Base.

I ended up working the front galley on this flight, which was not my usual position. Under the new request from Michael Deaver, I was putting this meal out which would cost $18.00 a person. This was double our usual meal cost.

As usual, we had other items on board in the event one of our passengers did not want the meal on the menu. The back-up food included what we needed to make sandwiches, salads and other similar, lighter items.

The galley where I was working was the size of about two phone booths. Here I was trying to get this fancy lobster dinner prepared in very limited space when Charlie walks up to me. He looked pretty intense.

"Do we have any corned beef? I need a corned beef sandwich," he said.

In the middle of my meal prep, I stopped and started looking. I had roast beef, ham, cheese, turkey; just about everything but corned beef. We usually had it on board.

When Charlie returned to check on the status of corned beef, I had to break him the news.

"Sir, I don't see any corned beef."

Still looking intense, Charlie said, "Let me see."

I wasn't offended at all because I knew he was under the gun. So, I took all the meats and sandwich material out, as best I could, around all of the Lobster Thermidor I was trying to serve.

Charlie scanned what I had and then mumbled something under his breath I can't repeat here regarding the fact that John Palmer, who had purchased the food for the front galley on this mission, had not bought any corned beef because he personally didn't like it.

"Well, just whip up a grilled ham and cheese sandwich," Charlie said.

It might sound easy if you were working in your home kitchen, but now I had to add a frying pan to the huge collection of food I was already working with in the two-phone-booth-sized galley.

After he served the grilled ham and cheese sandwich, I found out it was for Michael Deaver. The guy who put down the law for us to up the quality of food on Air Force One had ordered a $5.00 sandwich instead of the $18.00 lobster meal. That explained why Charlie was not a happy camper.

Later that night, when we were cleaning up the plane, I asked Charlie how he handled not having what Deaver wanted.

"What did you say to Mike Deaver about us not having any corned beef?"

"I said to him, 'Sir, I took a look at the corned beef and it didn't look good. How about a grilled ham and cheese?'" Charlie said.

United States Air Force CYA at its best. Obviously, at some point during Charlie

Palmer's Air Force career, he must have had his own "Coke bottle" moment.

While this one incident did frustrate Charlie, many of Michael Deaver's ideas about food on Air Force One ended up great. In fact, one menu item he came up with, an omelet featuring bacon and cheese, became known on board as the "Deaver Omelet."

Chapter Twenty

It was obvious President Reagan did his best to include his wife in his work and show her enormous respect and love. He even tried to make her feel better after what had to have been one of the scariest days of her life.

According to the Secret Service agents who were with the president when he was shot in Washington at the same time his press secretary, Jim Brady, was seriously wounded, Mrs. Reagan was at the White House. Despite their encouragement to remain there, she insisted they take her to "Ronnie."

As we now know, the wound was more serious than most people were aware of. If the bullet had lodged just another fraction of an inch we would have had another assassination of a president. However, when Nancy Reagan entered the room at the hospital, his focus turned to her.

"Honey, I forgot to duck," the President said.

It was not the only quip President Reagan made at the hospital. We heard that when he learned he was going into surgery for the gunshot wound he said, "I hope there are some Republicans in the operating room."

The president's recovery was quick, considering it was a potentially life-threatening wound. Before long, during a trip back to his ranch, he was chopping wood and working with his horses again.

One of his Secret Service agents who accompanied him to the ranch said, "If I had been shot I wouldn't be doing the things he's doing, working so hard." They were amazed over how energetic he was so soon after the attempt on his life.

I got news of President Reagan being shot while I was playing racket ball at Andrews Air Force Base with the presidential radio operator and a girl who was an administrative assistant to the pilot. We were trying to stay in shape to meet the demands of our job. When we heard what happened we were all worried and shocked. We were also very upset to hear about the serious injuries sustained in the shooting by the president's press secretary, James Brady. He was such a respected, capable communicator. Everyone was looking forward to many years of working with him and that had been cut short by the seriousness of the injuries inflicted by a mentally-deranged man trying to impress an actress, Jodi Foster.

The shooting of President Reagan and James Brady again brought to the forefront the seriousness of the work and the pressure on the members of the Secret Service detail assigned to protect the president. Not many forget seeing the image of the agents quickly forcing the president into the back of his limousine after the shots were fired.

Other than the Secret Service, the presidents themselves and their families, most people have no idea just how many death threats presidents get. The number is quite large. The more a president is dealing with emotionally-charged political issues the more the death threats come.

Mrs. Reagan was always very concerned about the president's security. It wasn't because she worried about herself or her financial security if something were to happen to him. She was just fine in that department. She simply wanted to spend more time with Ronald Reagan, her husband.

While some may think being on presidential detail as a Secret Service agent must be a great job, it is not among the favorite positions within the agency, according to agents I spoke with. They say the duties the agency is normally tasked with, counterfeit money, etc., is actually enjoyable and challenging. In that job they are playing mind games with sophisticated criminals. But, when they're working protective services for the president or other high-ranking officials they begin to use the same analogy pilots have used over the years – it's hours and hours of sheer boredom followed by minutes of pure terror. Basically, they are being paid to take a bullet to protect whoever they are assigned to.

One of the stories circulating in the media after the attempt on President Reagan's life involved General Alexander Haig, who was serving as Secretary of State at the time.

During the confusion following the shooting, the press was anxious to hear anything. At one point, Gen. Haig came into the White House press room and told them he was in control in the White House. While he accidently left out the speaker of the house in listing the succession of power, I believe he was taken out of context. There were a lot of behind-the-scenes issues going on during the event.

For one, then-Vice President George H.W. Bush was in a squadron plane, another 707, without secure voice capability on the aircraft. As a result, he was temporarily out of the loop.

I had worked with General Haig when he was a colonel serving on the staff of Henry Kissinger. I always thought of him as a very loyal, wise and meticulous man who looked at the big picture on issues.

He knew completely that the speaker of the house was in the line of succession, but just accidently left that position out in the heat of a very disturbing time. He was in charge as far as things at the White House were concerned at that time.

President Reagan's recovery was incredibly quick and he was back to work soon.

Chapter Twenty-One

When John Hinckley, Jr.'s shots were fired at President Reagan, he had been in office for only 70 days. Just a little over six months later, Egypt's president, Anwar Sadat, was assassinated during the country's annual Operation Badr victory parade.

President Reagan decided to send an impressive delegation to Sadat's funeral in Cairo, including previous presidents and dignitaries who had worked with him in attempting to seek peace in the Middle East.

Considering the guests on board the plane, it was definitely an historic flight. The delegation included former presidents Gerald Ford, Jimmy Carter and Richard Nixon. Others on that mission included Mrs. Carter, Dr. Henry Kissinger, Secretary of Defense Casper Weinberger and Secretary of State Alexander Haig.

It was an historic flight on an historic aircraft. This version of Air Force One, a Boeing 707 with tail number 26000, had been the plane that took the body of President John Kennedy to Washington after his assassination in Dallas. It was on that plane where Lyndon Baines Johnson took the oath of office to become the President of the United States upon President Kennedy's death.

The same plane also transported Senator Everett Dirksen, Vice President Hubert Humphrey, and First Lady Mamie Eisenhower to their final resting places.

There was probably more history on that plane than any other in the presidential fleet and now we were making more history. There was only one problem. Having that many former presidents and dignitaries on one mission created an enormous protocol issue. Where were we going to put all of these important people?

Of all the VIPs on board the plane, the highest-ranking, current office holder was Secretary of State Haig. As a result, he was in the on-board state room were the president would be if he were on board. Secretary of Defense Casper Weinberger was in the conference room with staff members.

With the special rooms occupied, this meant we placed the collection of former presidents and Dr. Kissinger in the section of the plane where the working staff would normally be on a routine presidential mission.

It certainly did not escape my attention that Secretary of State Haig, who once had been a subordinate of all of the people now seated in the staff area, including all the presidents and Kissinger, was now in the room that had served as the office of the presidents when they were in office. Is this a great country, or what?

At one point during the flight, as I was walking through the plane checking on our guests, Henry Kissinger grabbed my arm.

"Howie, you finally did it," he said. "You got me in steerage."

There were two legs on our mission to President Sadat's funeral. We first flew from Andrews Air Force Base to Madrid, Spain. We took a break, fueled up and then made our way on to Cairo.

With the exception of a few minor comments about our protocol problem on the flight, everything was going as smoothly as it could until nature called. The problem was that nature made its call upon too many at the same time.

It all started when President Carter got up from his seat in what was normally the staff area and made his way to the front of the plane. He approached me and very graciously asked if he could use the crew bathroom which was located just behind the cockpit.

Imagine that? The man I had once served as commander in chief was now asking me if he could use the crew head. In my personal book, that was history being made in itself. As I escorted President Carter to the crew bathroom, I was wondering why he would want to use the crew facility when there was a closer one to his seating area in the back of the plane.

It quickly became obvious to me that the former president chose this bathroom so he could avoid walking through the press area, which included the infamous Associated Press White House correspondent Helen Thomas. He likely wanted to avoid any questions as well as not be obvious that he currently did not have access to the private bathroom by the state room right now since Secretary of State Haig was in that part of the plane.

Everything was fine. President Carter was now in the bathroom of his choice and all was well. At least it was until just moments after Carter had entered the crew head up walked former President Ford.

"Howie, can I use the crew bathroom?"

"Sir, it's occupied right now," I said.

So, we stood there just chit-chatting while President Ford waited for President Carter.

Just a minute later, up walks Henry Kissinger. He walked right past us and up to the crew bathroom door only to see the occupied sign deployed. So, Dr. Kissinger approached President Ford and me and joined in the chit-chat. At one point he said, "Howie, discipline in the military is slipping."

"Why do you say that, sir?" I asked.

"Because all of you guys used to be scared to death of me," Kissinger said. "Now, it seems like you're not afraid of me anymore."

Before I could respond, Kissinger added, "Who the hell is in the bathroom?"

"It's President Carter, sir, and he took a book with him," I said.

"Well, yank his ass out of there," Kissinger said.

"Sir, I can't do that," I said, both of us smiling.

Now that would have been a story in itself if the chain of events had ended right there. But, just as Kissinger was finishing his challenge to me to remove President Carter from the crew bathroom, up walked President Nixon.

He stood there for a brief moment and assessed the situation accurately. He obviously concluded the crew bathroom was occupied and a line had formed. He turned to John Palmer, a flight attendant who had worked on Air Force One during his time in office, and said, "John, when it's my turn call me."

As Nixon walked back to his seat, I could only think that here was a collection of men who had served in positions as the most powerful men on the planet all waiting to use a bathroom while their former employee occupied their former office with his own private facility.

You can't make this stuff up.

There was another incident aboard Air Force One involving a bathroom I will never forget.

The bathrooms aboard the president's plane are a step above what you typically find on an airline. They are larger, have a nice mirror and a larger sink to place your toiletries and cosmetics on. Also, the actual toilet is underneath a cushion, almost like a small couch, that has to be lifted to access the head.

We once had the president of the People's Republic of China on board. The flight attendant assigned to him had forgotten to brief him and his aide on how everything worked in the bathroom. That became obvious by what I witnessed when I walked into the State Room when he was on board. Here was the leader of China, just inside the door of the head, being lifted by one of his aides and he was peeing in the sink! Talk about a breakdown in international communications.

Believe it or not, when I saw what was happening I didn't focus on what he was doing but on what must have been going through his mind. He probably thought, "This is a great airplane, but they don't have any place to go to the bathroom."

Chapter Twenty-Two

The respect by those who served President Reagan was not limited to those of us on Air Force One. We frequently heard stories by others who worked for the president.

Doug Holstein, who now lives in the same area of southeastern North Carolina where I do, is a former Marine One pilot. Marine One is the helicopter frequently seen in news reports that transports the president from the White House to Andrews Air Force Base for flights on Air Force One.

When it comes to getting the leader of the free world from point A to point B, nothing is left to chance. There is always a back-up. So, there is a back-up plane and a back-up helicopter.

Once, Doug was taking President Reagan to Andrews when, shortly after lift-off from the White House lawn and as they had circled the Washington Monument, something went wrong. Doug got a transmission warning light. That means he had to get the helicopter on the ground right away.

Any pilot's first job is to fly the aircraft. While he did that he also called into operations and instituted a plan B. They were going into

Anacostia where there is a Marine facility with a back-up helicopter.

Needless to say, lots of thoughts were going through his mind as he quickly taxied the helicopter to the back-up Marine One.

"I'm going to get fired, and the chief of maintenance is going to get fired," were a few of his thoughts. Everybody involved in the mission was sweating bullets.

When Marine One is secure, the back door opens and the Marine One security guard disembarks and goes to the front of the helicopter as the door opens. Down the steps come President Reagan and his staff. The president walked over to the back-up helicopter and stopped. He looked it over and then literally walked up to one of the tires and kicked it. He was obviously familiar with the aviation lingo of "Kick the tires and light the fire."

"It looks good to me, boys," President Reagan said. "Let's go catch an airplane."

Nobody got fired and that story made its way through the Marine Corps fast. Needless to say, he won them over pretty fast.

His respect for the military was obvious. He saluted every service man he passed. Stories of his respect for people who served America were common place. One in particular really moved me.

Despite being the iconic home of the president, some parts of the White House are simple and small. One of those areas is what is known as the medical annex. The Navy chief who was President Reagan's physical therapist told me that one day the President appeared in the room for an appointment. When he entered, he was carrying some papers and the Navy chief noticed Reagan appeared to have a few tears in his eyes.

"Sir, is everything ok?" the chief asked him.

"You know, they want me to give the Medal of Honor to this person," President Reagan said. "I just read what he did for his country. Who am I? I'm not worthy to give this man what he deserves."

It says a lot to remember that this emotion was not shown publicly, but in a quiet physical therapy session.

He obviously liked people in general. Before he walked off of Air Force One for a visit it seemed as if he had been briefed on even some personal things regarding the people he would be meeting or interacting with. If someone's child had just graduated from the academy, he knew that and he could talk to them about it.

There was a story I heard over and over, all over the country, from people who had met him along a rope line to shake hands with President Reagan.

"He seemed like he was excited to meet me!" they said.

It was a tremendous gift and I believe it was totally sincere.

President Reagan was a storyteller. He loved to share a good story or a good joke. Once, I remember him telling a story on the plane that looked like it may be going in a direction that seemed a bit off-color by his standards.

"You know, I have a good friend of mine, same age as me, who wanted to donate to a sperm bank," he began. President Reagan was well over 70 years old at the time.

"He went in and convinced the nurse he could do it despite his age," the President continued. "So, they gave him a jar and some magazines and put him in a private room. After about 20 minutes, they started getting concerned about him. Finally, after 45 minutes in there, he finally came out.

"My old friend said to the nurses, 'You know, I did everything I could. I ran it under the water. I even hit it on the side of the sink. But, I just couldn't get the lid off this jar.'"

He had us the whole time.

Based on the stories we would hear from Reagan's security detail, his visits to California were therapeutic. He loved the ranch and he loved to work on the ranch. By far, his favorites on the ranch were his horses.

He would shovel manure and work the horses. Then, he would chop wood and clear brush. He chopped lots of wood, because Nancy liked it hot in the house.

Imagine being the Secret Service agents assigned to protect the President of the United States, and the military aid standing there with the infamous "football," while the most powerful man on the planet shoveled manure and chopped wood because he wanted to.

Surprisingly, the little home on the ranch was certainly not a big one by presidential standards.

Obviously, what the Reagans liked about the ranch was the land. The house just happened to be on it. It was plenty of land on which the president could ride his horses and it was in his favorite state, California.

I also heard about a visit President Reagan made to the site of where they were building the Reagan Library. He was shown where he was going to be buried when he died. It was on top of a knoll in Simi Valley with a view down to the Pacific Ocean. One of the ladies giving him the tour said, "Aren't you going to have a beautiful view here?"

He looked, smiled and said, "It's always a good view in California."

Chapter Twenty-Three

After eight great years working for a genuine, gracious man, we now had a man from Texas heading for the White House. After the inauguration of George Herbert Walker Bush, who had been Reagan's Vice-President, we had one more flight with Ronald Reagan to take him home. The call sign on this flight was no longer Air Force One. We were "Executive Two-Seven Thousand," based on the N-number of the airplane.

As we were approaching California, I went into the on-board Oval Office where President Reagan was seated.

"Sir, would you like to come up front and make the last landing on the airplane with us?" I asked him.

"Yes, that would be great," he said.

I had invited him to sit in an observation seat in the cockpit for the landing.

On the planes that act as Air Force One, there is not a center aisle like you see on an airline. Instead, there are rooms built to either side of the plane. So, you walk down one side of the plane. As Reagan began to walk down the aisle along the windows, he stopped and started looking out as we began our decent over Orange County, California. Some of his staff looked out a window and I did, too.

"Howie, you want to see where all the Republicans live?" he asked me.

"Where is that, sir?"

"You see all those swimming pools down there? That's where the Republicans live," he said.

It was a sad day to take him home after working with him for eight years. It was a time period I enjoyed greatly and also meant a move up the ladder on the president's plane for me. I had gone from a member of the flight attendant team to Deputy Chief Steward under Chief Master Sergeant John Haigh on President Reagan's watch.

When you've worked with someone for eight years who served as the President of the United States, and you respect him like we did, we certainly kept up with the news and stories surrounding President Reagan after he left the White House. News that he had been diagnosed with Alzheimer's disease was heartbreaking.

Two years after President Reagan left office, and after his diagnosis had been made public, his Air Force One crew had the opportunity to spend about 45 minutes with him in his office. I have a photo that was taken during that visit of the President and me. He seemed fine that day.

About two years into President George H.W. Bush's term, we made a trip to the Reagan Library. The library was still under construction, but the decision was made to have a special pre-opening gala. The event featured Presidents Ford, Carter, Nixon, Bush and Reagan.

When we arrived, we were told our Air Force One crew would be accompanying the staff in the motorcade. This was very unusual. Leaving only the local security with the plane, we headed to the event in Semi Valley, California.

The ceremony was packed with people. A large number of them had made significant donations to the building of the Reagan Library.

In a once-in-a-lifetime opportunity, our flight crew was seated just to the left of the podium. We were about ten feet from the president and right next to Charlton Heston. This seating arrangement was obviously at the request of President Reagan and was yet another example of how well he liked the Air Force One team.

While no one really noticed, there had been a minor breakdown in communication regarding attire at the event. President Bush's valet had given him the wrong suit. He arrived wearing a light gray suit, while all of the previous presidents in attendance were wearing dark-colored suits. After President Bush had put his suit coat on, they also discovered it was missing a button. Someone was quickly tracked down to sew on a replacement. Traveling with the president is loaded with details.

At the Reagan Library event, President Reagan addressed the crowd. He talked about the potential of America. It was moving and motivational. By the time he finished his speech, you could sense the audience was ready to grab a shovel and shout, "Let's go!" It was classic Reagan.

Despite his diagnosis, it was obvious he kept his gracious demeanor and compassion for people as long as he could. I knew that because of an amazing story shared by John Barletta, who was a Secret Service agent assigned to him after he left office.

John rode horses with Reagan on the ranch, a favorite past time of his after his retirement. At some point, John noticed actions that indicated President Reagan's progressing disease was becoming a safety issue in riding. So, he first went to Mrs. Reagan.

"Because of the onset of the disease I believe it has become a serious safety issue for his horseback riding," John told her. "I think we should curtail this for his safety."

Mrs. Reagan told him he would have to be the one to break such sad news to her husband. Reluctantly, John approached President Reagan.

"Sir, because of the progression of the disease, I believe the riding of horses has to be curtailed for your safety."

Reagan looked sad. John instantly assumed this was devastating news to a man who loved riding horses as much as anything. He was shocked when the retired President responded.

"I know how hard it was for you to tell me that," Reagan responded.

Even at a moment where his disease had hit home possibly more than at any other time since his diagnosis and he was showing more compassion to the man who had to break the news to him.

To me, that speaks volumes about a man I had the pleasure to serve for eight years.

May this great man rest in peace.

Howie shakes hands with then-Vice President Ford
aboard Air Force Two. It was Howie's birthday.

Howie and Senator Ted Kennedy on the ramp.

Howie with President Ronald Reagan

Linda Franklin, President George Bush,
Barbara Bush and Howie at a
White House Christmas party.

A signed photo taken aboard Air Force One
with President and Nancy Reagan offering a
toast. Howie is in the rear of the photo.

Howie takes a break from duties aboard Air Force One
to visit with famous White House Dog Millie, who belonged to the
President George H.W. Bush family.

Howie (right) with actor Bruce Willis (center) and
fellow flight attendant Jimmy Saddler (left)
aboard Air Force One.

President Clinton talks with Howie and Linda
Franklin during a visit to North Carolina in
Air Force One. Howie is holding his son Adam, who
is now in the U.S. Air Force.

(Photo courtesy of *Star-News*, Wilmington, N.C.)

Chapter Twenty-Four

When my son, Adam, was eleven years old I took him to California to do a bit of sightseeing. One of our stops was the Reagan Library. This was after President Reagan's death.

I knew that the Boeing 707 that served as Air Force One during the Reagan years was being prepared to become an exhibit at the library. When Adam and I went upstairs at the library we could see outside. My old office, N27000, was sitting outside in some mud with the wings off, awaiting the building of the exhibit.

The paint scheme on this plane was not the familiar colors people are accustomed to seeing in the 747 version of Air Force One. This one was painted in Air Force squadron colors.

The next time I went to the Reagan Library, it was for the official opening of the Air Force One exhibit there. We were guests. The team that served the Reagans had been assembled for what was to be a very emotional event for all of us.

We were all placed on the plane in what were our usual working positions during the Reagan years. Then, President George W. Bush and his wife, Laura, escorted Nancy Reagan onto the plane, which was now the newest exhibit at the library honoring her late husband.

Charlie Palmer, who was my boss and chief steward during the Reagan administration, opened the door to let the Bushes and Nancy Reagan in.

As Mrs. Reagan approached the crew members when she boarded, she hugged us. It was a very moving moment and there was not a dry eye on the plane.

Years later, a big event was organized at the Reagan Library to celebrate the late president's birthday. I was honored to be asked to speak during an evening dinner the night before the actual date of President Reagan's birthday. It was a packed house.

I talked about what it was like aboard Air Force One during the Reagan years and shared many of the behind-the-scenes moments you are reading about in this book.

It was personally moving to me to be a part of the celebration of Reagan's life.

Chapter Twenty-Five

Usually having warm weather is about the only thing in common between Palm Springs, California and a favorite getaway of the new man in the White House, Beeville, Texas.

One example that quickly comes to mind happened on a trip to take President George H.W. Bush home over a holiday period. It involved access to food. During Reagan's visits back to California, there were all kinds of restaurants to dine in. Not the same in the part of Texas where we found ourselves. We were staying in George West, Texas. Its population was about 2,500 people and their claim to fame is being named the "Storytelling Capital of Texas."

It was New Year's Eve and Air Force One Presidential Pilot Danny Barr, a super leader, asked me if I could help find a place for the crew to eat dinner. The only place I could find was a dining area located in the back of a Citgo station. Sports fans, we weren't in Palm Springs anymore.

It ended up being a great night. The little restaurant was run by a Mexican-American family who had a lot of respect for the military.

In fact, one of the members of their family had been a Medal of Honor recipient. They treated us like royalty and the food was great. The cost was incredibly reasonable.

Everything was so good we almost felt embarrassed by what we were leaving as a tip. We wanted to tip them more than we paid for the meal.

When it came to feeding President Bush, we were fortunate to get some tips from the crew that flew him on Air Force Two during his days as Vice-President. We got a good briefing on feeding a president, Texas-style.

The schedule we received had us heading back to Washington from Texas, with a stop off in Alabama for President Bush to do a little fishing. So, I went out and purchased some Texas barbeque, along with coleslaw, hush puppies, baked beans and pecan pie. I had everything I needed to feed President Bush and the others that would be on board. I was ready.

I may have been good to go, but obviously things changed. I got a call from a member of the White House staff.

"It's changed," he said. "We're leaving at 7:30 in the morning, so we'll need breakfast."

On hearing about the schedule change, one of the crew turned to me and said, "Chief, what are you going to do?"

"Well, we'll store the pie and the coleslaw, keep the Texas bread out and I'll go buy some eggs," I said.

When President Bush boarded Air Force One the next morning, we were ready, again. We served him brisket, beans, eggs, salsa and Texas toast. He loved it.

The Texas barbeque acquisition was obviously a wise one. After his fishing trip near Birmingham, he got back on the plane and asked me, "Do you have any more of that barbeque?"

I think we served him barbeque all day long.

That trip revealed a big change between how President Reagan and President Bush's team handled schedules. While we would have a pretty good handle on our schedule up to three months in advance during the Reagan years, the Bush administration had a more fly-by-the-seat-of-your-pants approach. We learned quickly to expect changes at a moment's notice.

We flew more in the first six months with President Bush than we did during the entire eight years Ronald Reagan was in the office. In fact, his incredible travel schedule became an inside joke with the crew.

"Does this guy know he has a secretary of state to do this stuff?" we would frequently say.

I was discussing the schedule changes one day with Ray Shaddick, who was head of the Secret Service presidential detail. I had known him from the days of providing security for then-Vice President Spiro Agnew. He had worked his way up.

"He'll get into a routine," Ray said. "It will get better."

It never really changed. We had to adapt to the change in style. We just kept doing our job.

One trip that was particularly grueling was tough on all of us. The crew had already been working for five hours before we took off. There was lots of preparation behind a presidential trip. There was food to buy and store, plans to make and lots of details to handle. When we did take off we flew to Daytona Beach.

We sat on the ground for three-and-a-half hours in Daytona Beach while President Bush made a visit. When he returned, we took off and flew to Charlotte, North Carolina, where we were on the ground waiting for the president's return for two-and-a-half hours. A political issue arose while we were in Charlotte so we took the president back to Washington where we waited for three-and-a-half hours there. And remember, these periods were in addition to the flight times between the stops and we had been up since 3:00 o'clock in the morning!

The president returned to Andrews and we were quickly wheels up to Warsaw, Poland, for another almost ten hour leg! After sitting on the ground for five hours we took off from Poland and took him to Germany for an economic summit. When all was said and done, we had been working a 36-hour shift where the ground stops were as grueling as the flight legs.

At one point, the presidential pilot came out of the flight deck and approached one of our stewards, Mike Wiman.

"Mikey, do you have an aspirin?" he asked him.

"Sure," Mikey answered and proceeded to dump almost a full bottle of aspirin in the pilot's hand.

"What are you doing?" the pilot said.

Mikey certainly didn't intend to pour a bottle of aspirin in his hand. It was a result of fatigue.

Some people hardly put in 36 hours of work in an entire week. We had worked that many hours continuously on this one trip.

There were places to rest on Air Force One, but it was difficult to get serious rest time when you knew the president would be coming back at any time. In my case, I had become chief steward on Air Force One and was responsible for the whole airplane on a mission carrying the President of the United States. How can you rest knowing it's your show in such an important operation?

After we finally returned to Andrews Air Force Base, I had a talk with the flight attendant crew.

"Do you know how outstanding you guys are?!?!" I asked them. "You just put in over 36 hours and you all walked off that airplane and didn't kill each other. You were civil with each other and got along in a positive way."

I decided to emphasize my point by using an analogy.

"Let's say you are in a situation where I put you in a car with someone you are romantically involved with and you have to drive straight from Andrews to Disney World," I said. "You make the long 16-hour drive and you're beat. When you arrive, you would have to be careful how you talk to each other because of the fatigue. You guys did better than that and you aren't romantically involved. So, you're wonderful!"

When people were hired to serve on Air Force One we looked for people who were technically qualified. Of course they needed the skills to do whatever job they needed to do. But, it was equally important to find people that filled the same block you would hope to find checked on your child's report card in elementary school – "Works and plays well with others."

That was the type of crew we had on the plane.

These schedule changes we dealt with were probably second nature to President Bush. He was probably used to having things change midstream. He was the only president in recent history to run his own company for over 26 years. Having to make a course change was something he was likely accustomed to.

I quickly learned President Bush was not only a great businessman, he was a great family man, too. This Texas family was loyal to each other and very close. It was very common for his family to be traveling with him aboard Air Force One.

The family cohesiveness would repeat itself on Air Force One when his son became president. I had already retired, but a flight attendant working with President George W. Bush, Steve Lominac, relayed to me a story.

The president's daughters had just been all over the news after they had been allegedly caught drinking underage. His father, the former president, was on board the plane as the news broke. No matter what your politics are, you have to imagine how significant it must have been for George H.W. Bush to be sitting across the desk from his own son, now occupying the seat he once did.

Steve was in the room as the two Bush men talked quietly. Then, as the senior Bush got up to leave, the president said, just loud enough to be heard by Barbara Bush, "I think Mom would be the perfect person to talk to the girls about this drinking situation."

Before his father could respond, Barbara Bush said, "That's right. I'm going to take care of this. We're going to deal with this immediately."

As Mrs. Bush walked out of the room, President Bush's father turned to him.

"Good job," he said.

Chapter Twenty-Six

It was during the George H.W. Bush administration that we took delivery of the new, Boeing 747 version of Air Force One that had actually been ordered by President Reagan.

We picked up President Bush in the new plane after he had made a visit to the family compound in Kennebunkport, Maine.

After he boarded, he walked back to the press area on Air Force One and the press asked, "How do you like your new airplane?" He quickly pointed out he wasn't the one to order it so that he would avoid getting questioned about the expense.

The president's plane was frequently the subject of inquiries about its cost of operation.

I was once told it cost about $40,000 an hour to operate Air Force One, including the average aircraft cost, maintenance, fuel and the crew. While that may sound staggering, it is actually less expensive than if you chartered a 747, not to mention what it would cost to keep a crew on standby 24 hours a day, seven days a week and 365 days a year.

We were occasionally dinged in the press about the family-style, restaurant quality meals on board the plane. Whenever I heard that the press had brought this up, I always thought it was just them being sensationalistic in the media, especially when you considered what they paid for their meals versus ours if they traveled on a separate press plane.

Remember, everyone who flies on Air Force One is billed for their meals. It's not just some gift from the taxpayer.

During my days working on the plane breakfast on the president's plane was anywhere from $3.00 to $6.00. Lunch ranged between $4.00 and $7.00, while dinner was in the $6.00 to $12.00 range.

I would spend about $1,200 buying the food and contents to prepare meals on an average mission.

The press would pay for their meals on Air Force One as well. Plus, they would pay coach fare to fly on board.

If you compare that to the costs on a separate press plane that would follow the president on a mission, you see a substantial difference.

First of all, the press would pay three times what you would pay to fly first class on an airline to the same destination. Then, when it came to food, stewards working the press plane told me they would spend an average of $5,000 a day for food and materials to prepare meals on that plane versus the $1,200 we would spend on Air Force One. It's easy to see there is a big difference between the $3.00 to $12.00 cost of a meal on our plane and the average $30.00 meal on the press aircraft.

On some overseas missions the State Department would pay for the food served on board and you would see the quality of the meals increase.

On a few occasions I would get calls from the press about congressional trips taken on the plane. They would inquire about the cost of operation and meals on those trips. I would neutralize their inquiries easily by giving them an example.

"Go to Dulles and have a fresh fruit tray catered for four people," I said. "Then, go to a local grocery store chain and buy the same amount of fruit that a steward would purchase for our missions and see if there is a noticeable difference."

If they went to the trouble of following up on my example they would easily see a $90.00 difference just in something as simple as a fruit tray. The fact is that Air Force flight attendants save an enormous amount in operating Air Force One when you compare that to chartering a flight and catering the meals on board.

Back to the 747 version of Air Force One, I had always imagined a replacement aircraft during my days working on the 707s. I could easily envision a plane that would be bigger, more spacious and better laid out for efficiency in dealing with our type of missions. However, when the 747 came on line I could not imagine a better plane for the work. It does an incredible job for the President of the United States.

In conclusion about the plane, I've been asked how the Air Force One in the movie of the same name, starring Harrison Ford, compares to the real one.

While some of the plane's layout looks fairly similar to the film version, there are no "escape pods" like the ones in the movie.

I had learned during my days working for the senior Bush that his wife, Barbara Bush, was the cheerleader for the family. The family seemed to sincerely enjoy each other's company.

The Bush's loved to play sports with each other, but they didn't play just to have a good time. They played to win. As a result, President Bush would get impatient if things did not move fast enough.

For example, according to his security detail, if he went fishing he would throw his tackle out a few times. If he didn't catch anything he'd say, "Let's go to the next place." He liked to be on the move.

He moved fast on the golf course, too. He would play a round in two hours and 45 minutes. He accomplished that by hitting the ball and then literally jogging after it. He did that a lot.

I recall a trip when we took President Bush to Bermuda in the spring. The first day we were there it was sunny, but the winds were blowing about 20 to 30 knots. The temperature was 45 degrees. The terrain in Bermuda is very hilly. The crew played golf the first day, while it was sunny.

The second day, after the president had finished his commitments in Bermuda, he went to play golf with some of his staff. What a difference a day makes. Like the first day, the temperature was 45 degrees and the wind was up to 25 and 30 knots. But, this time it was raining. Late in the afternoon, they arrived back to Air Force One for our departure.

After everyone had boarded, Gen. Brent Scowcroft, an older, retired Army general who was then serving as the president's national security advisor, approached me.

"Howie, could you get me a cup of warm tea?"

Gen. Scowcroft was not a young man and he appeared chilled.

"Yes, sir, absolutely," I said. "What seems to be the problem?"

"You know, the man's crazy," the general said.

"Sir?" I responded, surprised.

"Absolutely!" he said. "We just played two-and-a-half hours of aerobic, aquatic golf and he liked it!"

On occasion the president's energy level would keep the Secret Service geared up. Agent Ray Shaddick shared with me that they really had to be on their toes during vacations with President Bush.

Ray related that once, when they were on vacation in the Florida Keys, the president got up early and wanted to go running. When President Bush was on vacation he usually didn't have a schedule. The president's position was, "When I'm on vacation, and there's no schedule, then the bad guys can't find out what I'm doing." That meant the Secret Service agents had to be ready for anything.

As he and the security detail were running along the shoreline, the president spotted a Coast Guard ship and decided he wanted to swim out to it to have coffee with their crew.

The last-minute decision to swim out to a Coast Guard vessel may have been a nightmare for his security detail, but it definitely showed President Bush's respect for the military.

On one occasion the Air Force One crew was invited to a Bush family Fourth of July gathering in Kennebunkport, Maine. It was a small family gathering with the Air Force One crew that ended up being not unlike any other family gathering in America. There were children's toys strung across the yard and a little tent for them to play in, too.

We assumed it was going to be a big event with the staff and others in attendance. We all were surprised to find it was just our crew and the Bush family. We were very privileged to be there during these special, private family moments.

At one point during the Fourth of July get-together everyone sang *America the Beautiful* and a there was a small fireworks display for the president. It was a moving, patriotic day.

Chapter Twenty-Seven

One notable Bush family moment occurred on Air Force One. On board the plane for the trip were President Bush's son and future president, George W. Bush and White House Chief of Staff George Sununu, who was the former governor of New Hampshire. One of George W.'s daughters, Jenna, was also aboard and had a loose tooth.

Anyone with children, or who recalls their childhood, knows that a loose tooth becomes an engrossing event to a kid. They are constantly wiggling it, touching it and looking at the tooth in the mirror. Jenna was no exception. She was anxious for this baby tooth to come out.

Gov. Sununu noticed Jenna's attention to the tooth. With her father standing in front of her, Gov. Sununu turned to the then-young Jenna and said, "You know, when that tooth comes out and you put it under your pillow, the tooth fairy will leave you two thousand dollars."

There was an extremely surprised look on her father's face, followed by everybody laughing.

At the end of the day, President Bush liked a massage. When the 747 was placed into service we had a massage table placed in the medical annex room.

When you enter Air Force One there's a private state room for the president, then the working state room for the president followed by a small medical annex. It had two bunks that would fold down from the wall. The medical annex also had a big chair and we would place the massage table over the top of the chair.

My concern was the massage table was not secured to the floor. I could just envision the president of the United States being tossed onto the floor of the plane while getting a massage after we hit some unexpected turbulence.

When my worries reached the maintenance team of the 89th, these guys, who could build an entire airplane from scratch if they wanted to, built a custom massage table for Air Force One that could be secured to the floor. We would set it up when the president requested it.

President Bush's desire for a massage became so routine that if we were on a mission with him on board, and we were in the air at the end of the day, I would automatically bring out the table and secure it in the annex without him having to request it.

On one trip the crew chief and I were in the process of securing the table when the president started getting on the table before we had finished the set up. I was in the middle of trying to get the sheet on the table, but he couldn't wait.

When he finally got situated on the table I put a pillow down near his head. He looked up at me and said, "Eat your heart out, Howie."

Chapter Twenty-Eight

While we had adapted to the fact that President Bush's schedule was a very fluid operation and could change in a moment's notice, there were some occasions when food became an issue. One involved a birthday cake. The only similarity in this incident and the one with President Reagan that left him covered in shaved chocolate is that the cake also came from the Watergate Bakery.

I was deputy chief steward on the flight and the chief, John Haigh, called me and said the president's appointment secretary had a birthday and I needed to serve the birthday cake on a campaign trip to New Hampshire. John was told the president had ordered this special cake for the appointment secretary. I was told serving the cake was tremendously important.

The campaign flight schedule called for a quick flight to New Hampshire, a layover of many hours while President Bush made an appearance, and then it was back to Washington. So, the plan was to serve dinner and the birthday cake on trip back to Washington. I had everything ready to go.

When President Bush boarded Air Force One I could tell he was tired. However, since I was told the birthday cake was important to him, I was still ready to serve it.

"Sir, I have the birthday cake you ordered for Mr. Farish," I said to him in the state room.

"Oh, it's his birthday?" President Bush said.

Immediately, I knew somebody was feeding somebody something, and it wasn't birthday cake. It was some wrong information about the importance of the cake that night. Seeing the president was so exhausted, I remembered my old friends, the Coke bottles, and I got us all off the hook.

"Yes, sir. I have the cake, but you look awfully tired. Why don't we just have John serve it on the trip tomorrow."

"That's a great idea," the president said.

Of course, the most publicized issue regarding what President Bush ate, or didn't eat, involved his dislike of broccoli. I was even part of the national news coverage regarding that one when some members of the press asked me about it. Looking back, I guess I sounded like a politician when I responded.

"I can neither confirm nor deny whether the president told me he disliked broccoli," I told them.

The fact was when we were briefed by the Air Force Two crew about President Bush's likes and dislikes, I just don't recall whether broccoli was on either list. Whatever the case, somewhere along the line his distaste for the vegetable made national news in a fun way.

"I don't like broccoli," he said. "My mother wanted me to eat broccoli, but I don't like it. I'm the President of the United States now, so I'm not going to eat broccoli."

The president's wife came to the defense of broccoli.

"I think broccoli is great," Mrs. Bush said. "I like broccoli. You ought to eat broccoli."

Little did I know at the time that all of this attention over broccoli would lead into the biggest scare I had when it came to feeding presidents on Air Force One.

We were on a Friday night trip bringing President Bush back to Andrews Air Force base. During the flight we had served vegetarian lasagna. Several hours from landing, the president's doctor came up to me in the plane.

"Howie, that lunch you served today with the vegetarian lasagna; did it have broccoli in it?" he asked.

"Sir, I'm not sure," I said. "But, I wouldn't be surprised."

I went to check the ingredients and, sure enough, it contained broccoli. I went up and told the doctor.

"You know, the president is allergic to broccoli," he said.

The range of emotions that hit me was astounding. First, I was afraid for the president.

Then, I felt surprised. Next, a little anger hit me because I thought I should have been told things like this since it was my job to feed the president when he was on board.

I turned to the doctor and said, "Sir, I had no idea."

"We know you're not accountable here," the doctor said.

I was still worried.

"Sir, he ate two portions of the lasagna and loved it."

The doctor looked at me and said, "Well, he's not doing very well."

Up until this point I had been focusing on wrapping up this mission for the weekend so I could make a trip down to Southport, North Carolina for a little R & R. Now, I'm being told the President of the United States is not doing well because of something I served him! Needless to say, my future was flashing before my eyes and I was sweating bullets. Then, it got worse.

I was summoned up to the flight deck. Presidential Pilot Col. Danny Barr wanted to talk to me.

"Did the doctor talk to you?" Col. Barr asked me. "I want you to know you shouldn't feel responsible. You're not going to be held accountable. We know that you didn't know about the allergy."

He sounded like he was trying to make me feel better. Maybe it did, just a little, until he followed all of that up with, "But, he's not doing well."

Now, my weekend trip to Southport was taking on a new meaning. It had gone from a chance to get away from work for a while to an escape from what had happened to the president under my watch as the guy responsible for what he ate on Air Force One.

Things went from bad to worse when I went to the doctor to check on President Bush. He had his doctor bag opened and was loading a hypodermic needle. He said he was going to have to give the president a shot to, hopefully, bring his allergic reaction under control.

By now, I'd gone from worried to really worried. I'm not doing well with this at all. I finally got the courage to go see the president.

When I walked into the door, President Bush looked at me and then hung his head low.

"I'm not doing well, Howie," President Bush said. "But, you don't have to worry about a thing."

Oh, my Lord! I was thinking.

After we landed at Andrews, two Secret Service agents helped President Bush to the door and off the plane. We stayed behind to clean the plane, but my mind was on what I had just seen and what had happened to the president because of food I had served him.

After our post-flight work was done, I hopped into my little Toyota to make the drive to North Carolina, knowing it would be a long, worrisome trip. As soon as I had left the base my cell phone rang. It was my deputy chief on Air Force One, Timmy Kerwin.

"Howie, the pilot needs to see you in his office," Timmy said.

Now, my nerves were really shot. The short drive back on base felt like forever and I was thankful that now I was chief steward, I had a parking place near the office of the presidential pilot. I took a deep breath and walked in. The entire crew was there and I just about panicked. I was thinking why would the whole crew still be here if something terrible had not happened?

My fear was obvious, but when my eyes landed on Col. James Jackson, he gave me the okay sign and laughed.

I had been had! Everybody was in on it. The crew. The president's doctor. Everybody! I had been the victim of a huge prank and the President of the United States was even in on the whole thing!

I had been known to be a guy who pulled other people's legs before, but this had been a masterpiece. So, I immediately thought about my good ole' trusty Coke bottles. I was so relieved that it wasn't true, but I didn't want them to think they had completely got the best of me.

"Oh, okay, you guys have been screwing with me," I said. "That's nice. That's a sign of affection. I'm going to Southport."

I walked out of the door smiling. I knew they were mad because I hadn't gotten mad.

What was going to be a miserable drive to Southport, North Carolina, ended up being a very pleasurable one.

After enough time had passed from the broccoli incident, I did get the chance to gain a tiny bit of revenge on a fellow crewmember.

You see, trying to do your best, even when you feel bad, is a benchmark of service on Air Force One. Everybody had a job to do and if you couldn't perform your job then things didn't flow as smoothly. So, I had this phrase I would shoot back if someone mentioned they were not feeling up to par.

For example, if we had been subjected to a grueling, 24-hour mission and someone on the crew walked up and said, "Boy, I'm tired," I'd shoot back with, "That's okay, you look good."

It didn't sound very sympathetic, but the crew knew what I was saying. We were a team and we all had to accomplish missions on behalf of the president, even when we didn't feel our best. So, we knew that on some days you just had to subscribe to the theory that it was better to look good than feel good.

On one mission, a fellow crew member, Jimmy Saddler, told me he wasn't feeling good. Before I gave my stock line of, "You look good," I stopped. I remembered that he was one of the guys involved in the let's-get-Howie-over-broccoli event. So, this time I changed gears.

"Man, Jimmy, you look pretty bad," I said. "I better get you back to the doctor."

On the Boeing 747 version of Air Force One, there was room to put an actual medical annex on board. I took Jimmy up there.

A short while later, I dropped by and the doctor was in there with Jimmy, who was now lying down on the bunk.

"Gosh, Jimmy, you look bad," I said.

"Yeah, I feel bad," he said.

Over the course of the next hour or so I had about eight to ten people drop in on Jimmy. They all told him he looked rough. Finally, I convinced President Bush to visit. He opened the door to the medical annex and said, "Jimmy, you look bad."

When the president chimed in, maybe Jimmy got a bit suspicious. Whatever the motivation, he jumped up and said, "I can't be that bad!"

He went back to work.

Operation Get-You-Back was a success.

Chapter Twenty-Nine

One funny and memorable event during the presidency of George H.W. Bush occurred during a trip to Bermuda. One of our relatively new crewmembers on Air Force One was a great lady named Wanda. She was actually from Bermuda where her father was a prestigious, well-known minister on the island.

On this flight, Wanda was returning to her home nation as someone who now worked for the President of the United States. The local people were very proud of her.

Air Force One landed in Bermuda and taxied to the staging area. When the door opened for President Bush to exit the plane, there was a large contingent of Bermuda citizens awaiting the arrival of the president's plane.

There were signs being held up all over the place welcoming Air Force One. However, there were significantly more signs saying "Welcome home, Wanda!" than there were welcoming the president.

When President Bush saw the signs, he turned to me and said, "What is this?"

"Wanda is from here, sir, and her father is a famous minister," I said. "They are proud she has come back home with you."

He thought it was wonderful.

With the fast-moving schedule involving President Bush, there had to be times where miscommunication would turn an innocent thing into something entirely unintended. That happened to a speechwriter for the president on one trip and it scared him half to death. It ended up being the equivalent of the experiment they would do in school where someone would whisper something in a student's ear and ask them to pass it around the room. The story had been completely changed before it was relayed to the last student.

In this case, the change came at just one level down.

The speechwriter was working with the president during his campaign for re-election. He would go to the front of the plane to speak with President Bush and then walk to another part of the plane to his work area to add material to the speech.

It became a back-and-forth mission for the speechwriter through the maze of Air Force One.

At one point, President Bush told another flight attendant, Timmy Kerwin, "Go ask the speechwriter to come back up here and I won't bother him anymore."

Timmy, who was juggling several things at one time when the president gave him the request, made his way back to the speechwriter. By the time he got there, the president's gentle request had changed into, "The president wants to see you and he says he's not calling you up there again."

Eventually, the actual version of the request came to light. When it did, the speechwriter told Timmy, "That was the longest walk I ever had in my life!"

The atmosphere aboard Air Force One among the crew was professional, but due to the serious nature of our missions we did use humor to maintain sanity. It was very much like a MASH unit. Yes, what you were doing was serious business, but you had to have a sense of humor in the balance.

Ask people who work in operating rooms in hospitals and they can relate. Things happen that may not be politically correct, but it doesn't change the professionalism of what is happening there. In fact, it increases the professional atmosphere by reminding everyone involved that in the big scheme of things, it's all about people.

Chapter Thirty

Another election had passed and another change was coming in the White House. While I was forming many memories of serving these men who were the most powerful on Earth, I also interacted with a series of many interesting people on Air Force One that did not occupy the president's seat. They ranged from celebrities, foreign leaders, military leaders, and other political figures to fellow flight attendants and crew members.

During one mission we had actor Bruce Willis aboard Air Force One. This was during the days people could not get enough of his film *Die Hard*.

I was talking with him and asked, "What was your favorite part of the movie?"

"The scene where I was picking glass out of my feet while I was saying, 'Come to California and enjoy yourself,'" Willis said.

It was not the last time I would see Bruce Willis. Not long after taking my position as director at Cape Fear Regional Jetport, he came to southeastern North Carolina to film scenes for *Return of the Jackal*.

One day they were filming at the airport. They were staging a scene that was supposed to appear as if he was jumping from a helicopter down onto a ferry.

It was a beautiful, September, California-type day when they were filming that scene. It was 76 degrees with a Carolina blue sky and low humidity.

When one of the film crew members came inside the airport I gave him a card and told him to tell Bruce hello.

After they had finished the scene, Bruce Willis came into the airport office, found me and said, "Howie! What the hell are you doing here?"

Since he and I had briefly talked during his flight on Air Force One about my plans after I would retire from the Air Force, he thought I was going to work for Marvin Davis of 20th Century Fox on his plane. That was my original post-retirement plan.

"I came here to poor man's California," I said.

He smiled and said, "You've got that right!"

Another celebrity I flew with I'll never forget was Mohammed Ali.

During those days he was well known for his flamboyant comments like "I'm the greatest" and "I dance like a butterfly and sting like a bee." After interacting with him, I concluded that was all showboat. He was simply smart and a great marketer.

His style worked and that's why Joe Namath copied it. So did Howard Cosell. Even ABC reporter Sam Donaldson would use Ali's remarks. They say imitation is the highest form of flattery. Ali was definitely subject to a lot of flattery.

Muhammed Ali was on a mission we took to Africa. It was during a time in his life when the disease that gripped him had yet to take much from him physically or mentally. He ended up being one of the most gracious guests we ever had on the airplane. He wasn't sappy, just genuinely appreciative.

In a style that reminded me of Ronald Reagan, he would always show sincere appreciation when we served him something. He made you feel important.

The galley we had on that plane was about the size of a bathroom. We would typically feed about 40 people out of that small area and guests on the plane would frequently comment when they saw the galley. They would say, "I don't know how you do this."

Ali was no exception. He made his way to the galley area during the flight and told me, "It's such a small place. How do you do it?"

Inspired by his well-known style, I looked at him and said, "And we're pretty, too!"

He laughed.

We frequently had some famous musicians aboard the plane. Once, the band Alabama was a guest and fellow flight attendant John Lewis Haig took them up to the cockpit to introduce them to the presidential pilot, Col. Barr.

As they approached the flight deck, John spoke to Col. Barr, who was in his left-seat position.

"Colonel, these are the guys from Alabama," John said.

Col. Barr said, "Really? I'm from Texas."

The Oak Ridge Boys and Lee Greenwood traveled with us a lot during President Bush's time in office. Greenwood had a huge hit at the time with his song, *God Bless the U.S.A.*

There were occasions where a function would take place right beside Air Force One. Lee Greenwood would kick off the event with his patriotic hit and the crowd loved it.

The president loved the music of the Oak Ridge Boys. Once, I entered the on-board state room where they were with the president. They were singing *Elvira.*

When the Oak Ridge Boys were on board I decided to have a little fun with a member of the crew. Phil Murphy was a flight attendant from West Virginia and he is a humble, laid-back guy. But he was really excited to hear the group was going to be on the flight. They were his favorite.

"You know they did *Elvira* and the bass singer used to sing for Elvis?" he said, in his excitement of hearing they were our guests.

He knew their entire history and repertoire.

Knowing how crazy Phil was about them, I decided I would ask them if they would make a big fuss over him.

When I went into the conference room to ask them about helping me make Phil's day, I found them looking through cabinets to gather souvenirs from Air Force One. I laughed.

"Hey guys, I've already got some goody bags put together for you," I said. "If you go through the cabinets I've got to replace all that stuff."

They laughed and I went on to tell them about Phil. They were in on the plan.

I went and got Phil and brought him to the conference room. When I opened the door every one of the Oak Ridge Boys jumped up, ran up to Phil, and made a huge fuss over him.

I sat Phil down at the head of the table in the conference room, where the president usually sits, and let him have a visit with his favorite musical group.

When his big event was over and Phil left the conference room, I walked up to him.

"Hey, Murph, you like your job?"

"Yes, sir!" he said. "I love my job!"

I had another opportunity to make another crewmember's day when two of the most famous baseball players in history were on board, Ted Williams and Joe DiMaggio.

Steve Lominac was relatively new on the crew. He was third in line to become chief steward on Air Force One and was named to that post near the end of the Clinton administration. He now lives in Oak Island, North Carolina, and is my neighbor.

While I didn't usually peruse the passenger manifest before a flight, the crew would look it over. When Steve saw the manifest, he called me in the back galley on the intercom.

"Chief, did you know Joe DiMaggio and Ted Williams are on this mission?" Steve asked me.

Before I could answer, Steve went on, "I don't know what I would do if I saw Ted Williams. He's my father's hero and he's my hero, too. This guy's bigger than any movie star. My knees would buckle if I met him."

I tried to bring Steve slightly back down to Earth.

"Well, you'll get un-star-struck working here and you'll learn to deal with VIPs on board," I said.

"I don't think I can handle this one, chief," Steve said.

Shortly after my conversation with Steve, President Clinton informed me, "Howie, you know we have Ted Williams and Joe DiMaggio on board. Would you make sure you give them a good show-and-tell of the airplane?"

I went to another flight attendant, Pat Andres, and asked him to take Joe DiMaggio on a tour and said I would give one to Ted Williams.

After taking Ted Williams all around the plane I wrapped up the tour in the conference room where I gave him a small box of souvenirs from Air Force One. It was obvious he was a real gentleman and a class act. Since I could tell he was an easy going guy, I decided to ask him to help me make Steve's day.

"We have a guy in the back fixing your lunch. He idolizes you. He's a great guy and he would think it was the best thing to ever happen to him to meet you. Would you meet him and make a big fuss over him?"

"Sure," Ted Williams said. "You've got to take care of the cooks."

"His name is Stevie," I said.

Stevie is something I called him. Everyone else called him Steve. I found out it wasn't his favorite thing in the world when I called his home one evening. His son, an older teenager, answered the phone.

"Is Stevie there?" I asked.

"Mr. Franklin, nobody calls my dad Stevie other than you," he said, laughing.

It hit me that Steve was a tough guy from Philadelphia who had achieved a security clearance only by the grace of God. Tough guys from Philly named Steve just don't like being called Stevie. He put up with it from me.

We had not yet departed on the flight so I made my way to the back galley where Steve was working on gathering the things he would need to fix lunch once we were airborne.

"Can you come with me just a moment?"

I led Steve to the VIP area on Air Force One where Ted Williams was waiting. He pulled off an Oscar-winning performance. Ted ran over to Steve and threw his arms around him.

"Stevie! How are you doing, buddy? It's so good to see you," Williams said, enthusiastically.

He had gone out of his way to make it seem Steve was a long-lost friend he was glad to run into again.

It was a major moment in Steve's life. He had actually met his hero. After he talked with Ted Williams a moment he began to make his way to the back galley to get back to work. As he is walked, under his breath, he said to himself, "I meet my life-long hero and he calls me 'Stevie.'"

Chapter Thirty-One

The diet preferences of the VIPs we flew on missions around the world occasionally seemed like the rumors you hear about what rock stars expect when they are on tour. There were missions I was part of in which green seedless grapes were flown in with frozen food and dry ice to meet the requirements of one of our passengers.

If food was important to our passengers there were a few missions when alcohol was flowing, too. Over the years there has been less alcohol consumed on Air Force One. However, there was a time where a lot of alcohol was consumed on board. One of the most memorable of those times involved the then-Speaker of the House Carl Albert. He was from Oklahoma and was known as "the little giant from Dixie," in reference to his height of five feet, four inches. I was told at the time he was the first Navy enlisted man to serve in Congress and he held the highest political office of any person from Oklahoma ever.

It was in the 70s and we were putting together a mission that would take Speaker Albert and a delegation of people from the White

House and State Department behind the Iron Curtain for 28 days.

Usually, on flights out of Andrews Air Force Base, we would buy enough food and pack it on the plane to avoid the necessity of making purchases or catering meals overseas. There was normally plenty of room to store the food on board. However, when I got a look at how much booze they had brought on board, I knew we had lost a lot of space and that we would have to cater meals once we arrived at the destination. I also knew this was going to be one of those trips.

While Speaker Albert was a nice guy and appreciative of the service we gave him, I don't think that he and a few staff members drew a sober breath on the entire trip. At one point, he and his wife got in such a dispute that she was transferred to a separate plane.

During another time on the trip, I was told by a State Department staff member that Speaker Albert had addressed a group of Communists while we were in Yugoslavia. Apparently affected by some drinking, he said to the group, "I want to thank all of you people from Czechoslovakia."

During the Carter administration, there was a Navy man named Lt. Commander J. Paul Reason who was a military aide to the president. He was the sharpest military aide I recall interacting with. He made decisions lightning fast and interacted very well with people. He was using the Total Quality Management concepts before anyone had ever put them on paper.

During a mission in Austria there was a cocktail party for the crew and he attended. At some point during the event I approached him.

"Sir, I'm not trying to kiss your butt or anything over a drink, but where did you get your management skills. I'm very impressed."

"When I got out of the Naval Academy I worked for this good captain," he said. "He taught me that there were good chiefs and there were bad chiefs. Find out who the good chiefs are and let them do their job."

His philosophy obviously paid off for him. He went on to become the first African-American man in Navy history to become a four-star admiral. He eventually became commander of the Atlantic fleet in Norfolk where he was the man in charge of more than 190 ships, 1,300 aircraft and 120,000 people at 17 bases.

Many of the high-ranking military people we would have on board were rightly proud of their accomplishments. This became a small issue on a flight I was working with Gen. Alexander Haig shortly after he made two-star. The mission took place as the Viet Nam war was coming to an end.

The plane we were on was a modified version of the KC-135/707 with executive seating on board. It was a nice aircraft, but we referred to it as the Air Force version of a Navy submarine because it had no windows. This was because it had been converted from its original use as a refueling tanker.

There were 16 seats and 16 bunks on the plane. It was originally designed to use for Defense Secretary Robert McNamara's trips back and forth to Viet Nam during his service to President Kennedy and President Johnson.

The trips with Gen. Haig would usually leave Andrews and make a stop in Alaska. Then, we would fly on to Japan for a stop before flying on to South Viet Nam. On some of those missions, we would have only four or five people on board.

On this particular flight, Gen. Haig was on a mission representing Secretary of State Henry Kissinger. He had a military exec on the plane by the name of Major George Joulwan who would eventually go on to become a four-star general and the supreme allied commander in Europe, a post held at one time by Gen. Haig.

When we landed at Yokota Air Base in Japan Maj. Joulwan noticed I was not flying the two-star flag.

"Gen. Haig is proud of his two stars," he said to me. "Why aren't you flying his flag?"

He was an aide watching out for his boss.

"Sir, we landed here in Japan as a Code Two," I said. Code Two is equal to the status of vice president of any nation. "We are in civilian clothes. Nobody here knows who we are. All they know is we are Code Two. With all due respect, sir, if I fly a two-star flag my priority goes right down the tubes."

"I understand," he said. "No problem."

He knew I was a crew member looking out for the boss, too.

One of the funniest breakdowns in communication I ever witnessed came when we had Ambassador Joseph Reed on a mission. I knew Ambassador Reed, prior to his days at the United Nations, when I worked at the Talisman Yacht Club. He knew everyone there. At that time he was the vice president and assistant to the chairman of Chase Manhattan Bank, working under David Rockefeller.

In 1981 he was appointed by President Ronald Reagan to serve as U.S. ambassador to Morocco, a post he held until 1985. Then, he served as chief of protocol of the United States at the U.N. from 1989 to 1991.

Ambassador Reed was a class act. Every time he traveled with us he would write a letter to the crew filled with compliments and thanking us for the service. Those letters helped me greatly in getting promotions.

During his last flight with us in his U.N. position, we were returning from Honolulu. He was on the back-up plane to Air Force One. He and his daughter were our only passengers on that leg of the trip.

Ambassador Reed came up to a fellow steward on the plane, Kevin Clark, and asked,

"Kevin, do you think I can take a picture back in the staff area?"

As a general rule, personal, unofficial photos are prohibited in the president's area of the plane. Kevin contacted the pilot to run the request by him, pointing out how kind the ambassador had been to us and did he see a problem with bending the rules this one time, especially since it was his last trip and the president was not on board. Plus, there was nothing classified in the area on this flight.

"Yeah, no problem," the aircraft commander said.

Kevin passed the good news on to Ambassador Reed who proceeded to head towards the staff area of the plane with his daughter.

After landing at Andrews, the pilot was standing just outside the door to the flight deck along with Kevin. They wanted to give a send-off to Ambassador Reed who had been so kind to us. As he made his way to the door with his daughter, they noticed the ambassador had a huge frame, at least 20 by 40, under his arm. He had taken a picture in the staff area alright, one right off of the wall of the back-up Air Force One!

This was a quick lesson in the "assume" breakdown. He had asked if he could "take a picture back in the staff area." The crewmembers were the ones who assumed he was talking about taking a photo with his daughter.

Initially, the pilot was very nervous over what the ambassador had done, but Kevin assured him the picture would be replaced fast. So, Ambassador Reed and his daughter made their way from their last flight on board with that picture they had taken, in the literal, not photographic, sense.

Chapter Thirty-Two

Those of us who served on Air Force One like to think we served everyone well and treated them like royalty when they were on board. There was one mission where I served some real royalty on the plane.

During the Reagan administration we had the Queen of England on a flight. We were taking her to California for a visit during a pretty rainy period.

The queen was everything you would expect her to be. She was very gracious, smart and astute.

When they returned to the plane for the trip back from California, the queen's husband, Prince Philip, the Duke of Edinburgh, made his way towards the back of the plane. He was taking everything in along with the two members of Her Majesty's Secret Service who had both served during the Falklands War. They were considered heroes because of their service during that war.

Prince Philip took notice of the photos of President Reagan throughout Air Force One.

"I see you're trying to stay in good favor with your boss by displaying his picture," Prince Philip said to me.

"Yes, sir," I said.

"I understand in four years that could change," he quipped.

He was obviously giving a good-hearted dig referring to the fact his position doesn't change in the United Kingdom.

As he walked away, one of the queen's security agents looked at me and said, "That's a wicked shot, isn't it?"

While Prince Philip noticed the photos in Air Force One, Queen Elizabeth noticed something else we had on board, Velamints. She fell in love with these diet mints we had on board that had become very popular in the 80s.

A neighbor of mine back at Andrews Air Force Base was married to a British lady. Her brother happened to be a steward for the Queen. Through that communication connection I got a message to me via my neighbor's wife from her brother.

"The Queen wants these mints and I can't get them in England," came the desperate plea.

So, for some time, I was involved in an, up until now, undisclosed smuggling operation. I would "re-appropriate" some of the Velamints from Air Force One and give them to my neighbor. His wife, in turn, would send them to her brother who would pass them along to Queen Elizabeth.

We were a bit hush-hush about the operation at the time, not wanting the press to find out about our smuggling arrangement. I was just behind the scenes, getting the job done for international relations, of course. I'm also thankful for the legal concept known as a statute of limitations.

Chapter Thirty-Three

THE PRESS

The majority of the crew on Air Force One did not have what I would call a real warm relationship with the press that traveled with us. For some reason, I did. Perhaps it was because I was from New York and could banter with them in their style. I think part of it was because I always had those proverbial Coke bottles in my pocket from my training days at Lackland Air Force Base. Those Coke Bottles allowed me not to take the press too seriously during our missions.

Some of the other stewards would watch Richard Valeriani, Ted Koppel and Marvin Kalb board the plane ahead of Dr. Kissinger during the shuttle diplomacy days. They would ask for a martini and maybe some nuts.

Under their breath, some stewards would say, "Who the hell are they?"

I'd tell them, "Just because they're riding in the back of the plane doesn't matter. If they ask for it, we try and get it. That's what we are supposed to do."

This all happened on a 34-day mission with Dr. Kissinger. I would occasionally have to push the other stewards to give the reporters on board what they asked for. They didn't like it, but their perspective was about to be changed.

After that grueling 34-day trip, Richard Valeriani wrote a letter to the squadron specifically praising the flight attendants. He didn't say the colonel and the boys did a good job, he singled us out.

I pointed out the generous letter to the other stewards.

"There's the guy you complained about and he was the only one who had enough gumption to write a letter that we can put in your promotion folder. Remember that," I told them.

The other advantage I had in dealing with media people was the fact I had worked as a flight attendant on missions with press on board prior to my Air Force One days. I had already traveled for years with reporters like Ted Koppel, Marvin Kalb, Bernard Kalb and Richard Valeriani.

I found it fascinating these guys were paid to use the English language to tell stories to the world. On board the plane, however, they passed the time by constantly digging on each other. It was their own version of MASH. Without using profanity, they would frequently tell each other to screw off.

On one flight, then White House press secretary Marlin Fitzwater was on board. He was one of the longest-serving press secretaries in history, serving six years under President

Reagan and President George H.W. Bush. Also on the mission was the infamous ABC News reporter Sam Donaldson, who had quite a reputation of being a no-nonsense, tough member of the press. Word had spread throughout the media that Donaldson had a new contract with the network paying him a million dollars a year. That was big money in those days for a reporter.

Marlin Fitzwater approached me and said, "Howie, see Sam Donaldson over there? He's making a million dollars a year now."

"No kidding," I said.

"You ought to go spill some coffee on him and say, 'Oops, I just spilled coffee on the Million Dollar Man.'"

I made my way back to the press table and there's Sam sitting with other reporters, including Helen Thomas. They were all drinking coffee out of these nice little plastic coffee cups.

I nudged the table just a little and said, "Oops, I almost spilled coffee on the Million Dollar Man!"

Sam smiled big, loving the attention.

"Wow, you're making a million dollars a year," I said.

"Yes, sir, I am," Sam said.

"I remember when you were making $250,000 a year," I said.

"That's right," Sam said.

"And I remember when you were making $500,000 a year."

"That's right, too."

I kept going.

"I even remember when we landed in California one time and there was a helicopter to pick up President Reagan and there was a helicopter to pick up Sam Donaldson," I said. "You were the only other person on the plane, other than the President of the United States, who had a helicopter come to pick them up and take them to Santa Barbara. And now, here you are making a million dollars a year."

"Isn't that incredible?" Sam said.

"Yes, it is," I responded. "But, I understand that Willard Scott is making two million a year."

"That goddamn weatherman!" Sam said.

I got the best of Sam Donaldson on another trip. He was sleeping and I woke him up.

"Sam, you need another pillow?"

"Howie, I won't screw with you if you won't screw with me," he said.

When I first became a flight attendant on Air Force One, a fellow crew member told me, "You take care of Helen Thomas."

"Why's that, sir?" I asked.

"I got in trouble one time and she got me off the hook," he said. "I got a DWI back in the Nixon days. I could have been kicked off the crew. She went to the Colonel and said, 'If you fire him I'm going to eat you alive.'"

Because of Helen's intervention, his punishment for his DWI, as far as service as a crewmember was concerned, was he ended up flying as a flight attendant on a Jetstar for a few months.

For eighteen years on Air Force One, whether I was on board or not, I made sure the infamous Associated Press White House correspondent Helen Thomas had half-a-cup of black coffee when she walked on board the plane. That's what she wanted.

It was during watching Helen Thomas write her stories that I realized the entire press were two-fingered typists. It seemed like a mark of the trade. She typed with two fingers.

Marvin Kalb, while writing his copy in preparation for his stories on the CBS Evening News with Walter Cronkite, was using his two fingers. Ted Koppel? Yep, two fingers.

Once, while Marvin Kalb was working on a story, I said, "Two fingers?"

"Yes," he said. "That's $250,000 a finger."

Helen Thomas would eat just about anything we would serve her on the plane, even though she did try to stay on somewhat of a diet. She loved bologna sandwiches. It had to be a really good, deli-sliced bologna. Put a deli bologna sandwich in front of her and she was a happy lady.

Helen Thomas was often referred to as the "Dragon Lady" because she would go right for the throat if she thought she had a question that needed to be answered. In my opinion, she asked questions that were pertinent, without getting too personal. She was definitely tough. She was such a staple of the White House press corps that it was a tradition she would get called on for the first question by the president or his press secretary.

She actually retired twice. The first time she wrote a book titled *On the Front Row* about her experiences covering the White House. Since she had known me in my role as a flight attendant for 20 years she called me and did two, two-and-a-half hour interviews with me.

There were several pages in that book that refer to me. But, she got 50 percent of it wrong. From that experience I learned to be careful believing everything you read in the press.

I spent so much time working on the plane with Helen Thomas that I used to joke that she and I had slept together – in the fuselage of an airplane that is. I had seen her without makeup.

Chapter Thirty-Four

Food and fancy clothes did not mix well with Andrea Mitchell of NBC News on one flight. She always wore nice clothes.

During the Reagan administration we were flying out of California serving what we called the "California breakfast," consisting of sausage, eggs and hash browns. The sausage was a large, fresh country sausage as big as many Italian sausages.

When Andrea Mitchell cut into her sausage grease streamed out and made a beeline right for the middle of a very nice, beautiful red silk blouse she was wearing. To say she was not a happy camper would be an understatement. She was very upset and, putting it diplomatically, she expressed herself strongly about the incident.

I don't want to write specifically what she said, but I would imagine any sailor on board would have been impressed.

She would also complain about the tables in the press area of Air Force One not being clean. However, the fact was it was the fault of fresh newspapers they expected on board.

The tables in that section would fold up to allow seating for flight. When the press was boarding the plane, the tables would be down and we would have copies of the *New York Times* and the *Wall Street Journal* on them. Since they were hot off the press, ink would leave marks on the table.

When Andrea Mitchell would board and pick up a paper, she would say, "How come you don't clean the table?"

Sometimes you can't win for losing. We would just smile and clean the newsprint off of the table for her.

While Ms. Mitchell wore nice clothes, she was not voted the best dressed correspondent on board by our crew. That honor went to Ed Bradley of CBS News, who would become a popular correspondent on *60 Minutes*. He was a sharp dresser and even dressed better than the president! He was a tremendous gentleman.

During one mission, Ed Bradley strolled up to me on the plane.

"Howie, where are you from?"

"Sir, I'm from Long Island," I said.

"I thought so. I could hear that accent," Ed said.

"Yes, sir, I'm trying to lose that accent."

"Don't do it!" he said.

"Why's that, sir?"

I'll never forget his response.

"Because that's who you are," he said.

Ed Bradley was in a class of his own, a gracious man.

Tom Brokaw, who would go on to become the anchor of NBC Nightly News, was another member of the press we would have on some flights. He was a gentleman when he was on board and always seemed very appreciative of the service we would provide to him.

I did get to see a part of Tom Brokaw that I don't believe any of his TV viewers knew about. Believe it or not, he had long hair in the days as host of *Today*. During a trip to Vienna, Austria, I saw him jogging and his hair was flowing in the wind. His hair was not down to his shoulder, but it was much fuller and longer than viewers saw. How he concealed it while he was on the air, I don't know.

Another alumnus of NBC News we had on board was Katie Couric. She was on board to interview President George H.W. Bush.

I went back to welcome her in the VIP guest area of the plane. During our conversation I shared a story with her about her predecessor, the co-anchor of the *Today* show, Barbara Walters.

Barbara was on board a mission I was not assigned to, but was told about the story. She was on a flight out of China and was not impressed with what was on the menu for the flight. One of the stewards prepared a Spam sandwich for her.

The next morning Barbara told the world, on the *Today* show, that she was served a Spam sandwich on Air Force One.

There was actually a very good reason for having to serve her a sandwich using canned meat. In those days there was no refrigeration on Air Force One. All the food we carried on long, overseas flights had to be frozen or canned. Since we would have about seven days' worth of food on board, it was a challenge without refrigeration. There were obvious reasons for not venturing out to a local market in China to buy food for Air Force One.

There was certainly no attempt to low-class Barbara Walters on that trip. There were simply serious limitations on that flight to China.

Another press incident on Air Force One revealed the importance of attention to detail on a mission.

Tom DeFrank, who spent 25 years as the senior White House correspondent for *Newsweek* magazine, was on a mission where we were taking President Reagan to China.

As usual, we took a rest stop in Hawaii. On the flight, trying to set the tone for heading to Hawaii and China, we served pineapple with chicken salad. While we were out buying food for the trip we also bought some chopsticks and put them out on the tables. The people working the front of the plane took the wrappers off of the chopsticks before putting them out. The guys in the back of the plane left the wrappers on.

Tom DeFrank, in the back of the plane with the press, picked up his chopsticks and read the label.

"These are Taiwanese chopsticks," he said.

Believe it or not, that made *Time* magazine. To me, it was a non-story. After all, where would you be able to find chopsticks made in Communist China sold in Washington, D.C. at the time.

It would have probably never made the news if the wrappers had been removed from the chopsticks in the back of Air Force One.

Another media figure we would occasionally have on board was conservative writer and commentator William F. Buckley, Jr. I can't think of any other member of the press that was well known by their entire name, including the "junior" at the end.

The first time I met Buckley we were on an around-the-world squadron trip with then-secretary of the Navy John Chafee, who would later become a U.S. senator. We were traveling on a 135, which is a Boeing 707 with no windows. It was the plane we called the Air Force version of a Navy submarine. Buckley was on board while we were traveling to Australia.

Since I consider myself kind of a conservative guy, I liked Buckley. I usually liked what he had to say and I was fascinated by his unusual accent.

One very noticeable thing about Buckley was his clothes. Everything he wore seemed to be always wrinkled. His pants, shirt, jacket and even his tie were all wrinkled. That was something someone obviously corrected prior to any of his television appearances.

I also noticed when he would read a book he would put on headphones. We were having a conversation once and I asked him about it.

"What do you listen to in your headphones?"

"I listen to fast classical music," Buckley said.

"You like that music?" I asked.

"I read faster," he said.

When we arrived in Australia, Sec. Chafee and his guests were leaving to go on a tour. Buckley got half way down the steps and turned to come back up. He entered the plane and picked up a book he had been reading.

He looked at me, held up the book, and said, "I need this in case things slow down."

On another trip, Buckley was a passenger on Air Force One. This time, his wife was with him and she was dressed very nicely and neatly. Buckley was his usual disheveled self. It looked like he had slept in his clothes. I always found it interesting that this well-known man seemed totally unfocused on his appearance. It just obviously was not very important to him to be neat. In fact, when he would read a newspaper on board he would leave behind a wadded-up ball of paper.

Buckley was an intellectual, class act. Perhaps he had so much going through his keen mind at any one time he just paid no attention to things like what condition his clothes were in.

Chapter Thirty-Five

The Crew in Blue

You don't work with a tight-knit crew as long as I did without ending up with a boatload, or should I say planeload, of memories about them.

I could write an entire book just on a fellow crewmember named John Lewis Haigh. When I was relatively new on board and considered the fourth man in line, he was the number three flight attendant on Air Force One. So, he was my boss.

John Haigh has a laugh that's so impressive I believe they would pay him in Vegas just to sit in the audience of a comedy act. If you happened to be sitting in a movie with him when a funny line was delivered you would laugh at the line and then laugh even harder at hearing John laugh.

We would actually pay John's admission to get him to go to a funny movie with us. Once, in Palm Springs, they actually threw us out of a movie theater because we were laughing so hard.

Since I've been in my new position as airport director in Southport, N.C., I've put a man who works at the airport, Jimmy Mock, on the phone with John to tell him a joke. Jimmy burst out laughing after sharing the joke with John. He wasn't laughing at his own joke, he was laughing over John's famous laugh.

Of my many memories surrounding John Haigh involved our constant quest to keep everyone happy on board as far as the many different diets our passengers would be on at the time. Some top political people seemed to be on a perpetual diet.

Nelson Rockefeller is just one example. He was one of the richest people in the country during his day. What did he eat? It was usually green, seedless grapes, celery and carrot sticks. He was just one of many people who had reached a point in their life and career where they could eat anything they wanted, but they just could not afford to eat what they wanted from a physical standpoint.

Marlin Fitzwater, who served as the White House press secretary for six years, under both President Reagan and President George H.W. Bush, liked his food. He would take breaks from his usual eating habits by going on a rotating Slim Fast diet.

Once, he told me, "I drink this stuff for six months and lose my weight. Then, I eat for two years."

On one trip, Mr. Fitzwater was on his Slim Fast diet and ordered a Slim Fast shake. John Haigh asked another flight attendant, Timmy Kerwin, to get the Slim Fast.

Timmy pulled out the container of Slim Fast and began to shake it up. John apparently thought Timmy wasn't shaking it fast enough so he took it himself and began shaking the container really fast and hard.

At one point, in mid-shake, the lid came off and Slim Fast went all over John. It was literally dripping from his glasses and running down his sport coat.

John looked at me and said, "Don't laugh."

It was an order I knew I couldn't comply with, so I said, "I'm outta here."

All of us loved going on trips to California. We would frequently stay at a great hotel owned by Princess Cruise Lines. We would have breakfast at the marina and, when time allowed, play golf and racquetball. They would give us four drink tickets at night. We would also have access to a rental car.

Since I was more of a home guy than others on the crew, I would sometimes volunteer to stay back at Andrews Air Force Base and take my duty time in the office. One day, I had to contact John Haigh with some information. It was 7:00 a.m. in Washington and 4:00 a.m. in California. I did not know that John had been out very late the previous night and had not been back in the hotel for long. He had just gone to bed.

In his case, my call came not at the break of dawn, but at the "break of dark." It was obvious he was half asleep when he answered the phone.

"Hellloooo," he said, very weakly.

"You gotta pee?" I asked.

Sleepily, John said, "Yeah."

"Well, go pee," I said.

By the time he returned to the phone John was awake enough to now realize just what had transpired.

"Franklin!" he shouted into the phone. "The next time I've got to pee, don't call me!"

That call remained in the repertoire of Air Force One crew stories for a long time. Years later, when I had become chief steward on Air Force One, a side trip that was going to take place in a Gulfstream jet had popped up on orders from the White House. It would be my job to staff this last-minute mission with a flight attendant, so my phone rang at 3:00 o'clock in the morning. It was Col. Danny Barr, the presidential pilot, on the phone.

"Franklin, you gotta pee?" he said. "Well, go pee."

Karma is tough, but I wasn't about to be the last guy in line. Now, I had to pass the news about this pop-up mission to the head of airlift operations at the White House and former Air Force One flight attendant, Denny Stump. By now, it's 3:30 a.m. and when he answered, you guessed it, I asked him, "You gotta pee?"

One of John Haigh's claims to fame was; how do you put this delicately; when he had to go, he just had to go. His bowels just didn't like delays when the entire digestive process had taken place.

We were traveling to a hotel out of town when John made it clear he needed to get to a bathroom fast. We he arrived at the hotel, he grabbed his key and went flying down the hall to where he thought his room was, only to find the door already open. So, he flew in and let nature take its full, glorious course. There was just one problem. It wasn't his room. Either the person in the room had just checked out, or had stepped out for a moment and left the door cracked open. When we found out about him being in the wrong room, we asked him about it.

"You just used another guy's bathroom?" I asked.

"I knew something was wrong because that piece of paper they usually put over the toilet wasn't there," John said. "I'm just glad it wasn't a trucker in the room or he would have thrown me over the balcony."

When you have a crew that worked in the close-proximity and in long duty times like we did, political correctness would sometimes fly out of the window.

The guys on the plane created this modified, one-to-ten system in rating ladies we saw. We were very conservative. It only took a three to be one you would be willing to bring to an Air Force One Christmas party. A six was dynamic, a Miss America type.

Once, John Haigh told us he had just met a lady he gave a nine-and-a-half.

"A nine-and-a-half!" I said. "What warranted that?"

"She spoke to me," John said.

On one mission, John had a high-ranking member of the government of India on board. This guest was big on health and his faith. He had a limited amount of food he would eat, so John went down to the embassy to ask about food he should prepare.

When John returned from the trip, we asked him about the mission.

"Well, at first we thought he was Unitarian," John said. "Then, we thought he was a vegetarian. In reality, he ended up being a hemorrhoid."

The occasional lack of political correctness was not limited just to the male of the species on some of our trips.

On some missions we would have Army nurses on board the plane. These ladies were 100 percent, top of the line, in professionalism, image and personality. So, imagine how shocked I was when one approached me on a flight and said, "Howie, do you know why God created martinis?"

"Why is that, ma'am?" I asked.

"So ugly women can get laid," she said.

Another member of our crew was Kevin Clark. He received an education of just what our job could mean on a flight with Secretary of State George Schultz on board. Schultz, who was serving under President George H.W. Bush, had requested some cashews from Kevin. He tracked me down on the plane.

"The secretary wants cashews," he said. "I looked and we don't have anything but mixed 'nuts."

"Well, pick them out," I said.

Kevin was a scratch golfer. We had a trip scheduled in a Gulfstream to take John Sununu, who was President George H.W. Bush's chief of staff at the time, to Palm Springs. The crew really liked Sununu and he had a great sense of humor.

Since I knew Kevin would love the opportunity to play golf in Palm Springs, I told him he should get on the trip. He liked the idea. I told him to make sure he went to the renowned Morningside Golf Course.

"Take a deck of playing cards from Air Force One with you and give them to the pro," I told Kevin. "He'll hook you up."

While in Palm Springs, Kevin went to the course. The pro said he had something going on at that moment and he should return around 1:00 that afternoon. When Kevin returned the pro said, "I've got you lined up for a free round with this guy named, Sue, ah Sue something, and his wife."

He had been paired to play golf with the chief of staff, John Sununu! Here's a guy who was a steward on the plane and now he ends up playing a round of golf with an important

Washington political figure at a prestigious golf course in California.

While good golfers can occasionally get temperamental, Kevin remained calm during the round and played a good game of golf. From Sununu's perspective, here's the guy that was waiting on him on the plane and now he's playing scratch golf with him.

Near the end of the round, Kevin sank a long putt. Sununu turned to his wife.

"Now I know what the boys on Air Force One do when they're not flying," he said.

Another member of our team on Air Force One was Steve Lominac, who has a very outgoing personality and was the guy who I had Ted Williams make a big fuss over. Steve never meets a stranger.

Once, we were on a mission to Moscow. Steve had been into the Russian capital before on squadron trips and was much more familiar with the place than we were. He was accustomed to making frequent overseas trips in his previous Air Force work, while we only went across the pond maybe twice a year.

After arriving in Moscow he took us to a bar. We were pretty nervous about venturing out in a Communist country, but it was obvious that Steve had been there and done that. He was comfortable and knew his way around Moscow.

When we walked into the bar the bartender looked up, saw Steve and shouted out, "Whiskey and fresh horses for my men!"

Steve had definitely been there before. It was a phrase he had spread all over the world.

While Steve Lominac's "Whiskey and fresh horses for my men," became well-known around the world, I guess I can take credit for one of my stock phrases becoming a cliché on Air Force One.

Many times I would be serving a high-ranking official on the plane and they would comment on me doing something for them they considered above and beyond the call of duty.

"Sir, all I want to do is make you look like a star. If I make you look like a star the only thing I ask in return is you throw me some crumbs and drag me along behind you," I would say.

One of the pilots who served as a first officer on the flight deck was Col. Belsito. I was doing something for him and he said, "Chief, you don't have to do that."

I responded with my stock, make-you-a-star comment.

During the George H.W. Bush administration, I was on a flight to the president's retreat in Kennebunkport. Col. Belsito was the commander on the flight. Before the president and his staff began to board, I looked down the steps to see Col. Belsito grabbing some of the classified cases to bring them up the steps. I quickly intercepted him because it was certainly not the duty of the presidential pilot.

"Sir, you don't have to do that," I said. "Let me handle it."

Col. Belsito looked me in the eye and said, "Howie, all I want to do is make you look like a star. If I make you look like a star . . ."

Chapter Thirty-Six

The chief of security on Air Force One was an African-American man named Hoyt Gamble. He would later go on to become chief of security at Andrews Air Force Base.

When Hoyt Gamble became chief of security on the plane, I asked one of the men who worked for him what he thought of his new boss.

"Are you kidding? I'd do anything for Chief Gamble," he said. "That's a man."

He went on to compare his new boss with his old one.

"I'd get called in because I did something wrong and I would walk out of his office feeling so low about myself for what I had done. I'd also feel low about myself for allowing a man to talk to me that way," he said about his previous chief.

"When I go in and get my butt chewed by Chief Gamble, he tells me what I did wrong, what to do to get it right, and then he tells me how good I'll do it from now on. I walk out feeling better about myself than I did when I walked into his office."

Obviously, Hoyt Gamble was good at what he did and was respected by the people who served under him.

I also liked Chief Gamble a lot and confess that I would mess with him on occasion, much like our stress-relieving MASH antics on board. One routine thing I would do just drove him crazy.

As head of security, he is the man in uniform at the base of the steps when the president exits Air Force One. Chief Gamble always looked professional in his uniform. In almost all news footage of the president getting to the bottom of the steps, you see him, standing at attention, at the bottom of the steps.

It caught my attention that you always saw him from the waist up. So, I added a little after-landing item to my routine.

When Air Force One landed and was chocked I would usually take the president's luggage on the plane and transfer it to Marine One. It would be about that time the president would exit the plane.

So, my new routine became put the bags on Marine One and then make my way back to the plane and stand right beside Chief Gamble in my steward uniform. As I stood right beside him, I'd reach over and take his hand in mine.

What could he do? He was at attention with the cameras rolling. He couldn't reach over and hit me.

Every time I did it he would say," Franklin, don't do that shit! You're making me feel really insecure here."

Speaking of my duty of transporting suitcases from Air Force One to Marine One, there was one occasion when things did not go quite as planned and the incident earned me a new nickname.

The protocol upon landing at Andrews Air Force Base would be that Air Force One would taxi up to Marine One and stop perpendicular to the helicopter in order to transfer the president and others that would be accompanying him to the White House. During the process, I would take the bags and place them on Marine One.

There are steps at the front of Marine One and steps in the rear. The president always entered using the front steps and I would use the rear steps to load the luggage, which I would place in the right rear of the helicopter behind a mesh cargo strap.

It's worth noting in this story that flight attendants dressed in civilian clothes and not military uniforms. There are many reasons for this including projecting more power than our rank gave us when we had to tell a senator or other high-ranking official to return to their seat and buckle up. Because of the attire I wore, it was possible I could blend in with the "suits" accompanying the president. That's obviously what happened on this fateful day.

I was on the helicopter securing the luggage in the cargo area and was apparently blending in with the staff members standing around in Marine One, making it look like a New York subway. Before I could make my way to a Marine One crewmember to exit the helicopter, I heard doors shut and the "whoop, whoop, whoop" of the rotor blades starting to turn.

The presidential pilot, still on Air Force One, as well as the rest of my crew, could see I had not exited the helicopter.

I fought my way to the front of Marine One where I saw a Lieutenant Colonel and the president.

"Howie, you're not supposed to be on here," the president said.

"You're right, sir!" I said.

"Are you going to the White House with us?" the president asked me.

"Not if I can help it," I said.

Next thing I hear is the sound of rotor blades slowing down so I could get off of Marine One and keep from having to explain how I ended up on the lawn of the White House.

Still watching all of this transpire is the crew of Air Force One. Now, they see the blades come to a stop. The door opens and off walks me.

That incident earned me the nickname, "Helicopter Howie."

By the way, just like Air Force One, the helicopter is not referred to as Marine One unless the president is on board.

Col. Danny Barr was a well-respected presidential pilot on Air Force One. He was a great commander. He was the guy in charge of the plane when he was on board. Once, a presidential aide put me in an awkward position when he did not follow the chain of command.

It happened while we were on the ground in Newark, New Jersey. President George H.W. Bush was at the United Nations giving a speech. We had flown him to Newark and Marine One had transported him to the U.N. headquarters.

We had televisions on the plane and the big news was that Hurricane Andrew had made landfall in Miami, Florida. It was a devastating storm doing substantial damage. We knew the president would want to go there to survey the aftermath and offer federal assistance to the victims.

There was one problem. Our flight plan just called for the trip to Newark and back to Washington. So, the only thing we had left on board in the way of food was snacks. I had already started to make some preparations to get food in the event our speculations came true. I called the advance officer for the mission.

"Please find me a nice place to buy food, a good grocery store," I requested. "Also, I need to know how to get there and I need transportation to get there and back to the plane."

Before I heard back a military aide, who was on the advance team and had arrived in Newark the day before, came booking up the steps to the plane.

"Who's Howie?" he said.

"I'm Howie, sir, what can I do for you?"

"The decision has been made that we are going to Miami to see the damage from Andrew," the military aide said. "The president said 'Somebody has to tell Howie,' so I knew I had to come meet whoever Howie is."

I looked at Col. Barr, who was standing with the crew.

"Can I go shopping?" I asked.

Understandably, Col. Barr is a little taken aback. This was an obvious break in the chain of command. Col. Barr, as the presidential pilot, is the commander of Air Force One and the man who needed to know first and foremost of any changes. This aide, based on a comment from President Bush, had thrown all of that out the window to seek a steward on board.

"What am I, chopped liver?" Col. Barr said.

"So, can I go shopping?" I pressed.

"Not until I give the official word," Col. Barr said.

We just sat there a few minutes. Finally, Col. Barr spoke up and asked me, "How much time do you need to go shopping?"

"I needed the last three minutes, sir," I said.

"Get the hell out of here and go shopping," Col. Barr said.

For such a last minute situation, the meal we prepared for the Florida trip became a hit. We went out and quickly bought some chicken, vegetables and some sauces. Preparing the food in the back galley was a flight attendant named Vance Makanui. He was from Hawaii and a great cook. He put together this seasoned chicken breast with vegetables meal.

After we served the meal, Senator Connie Mack of Florida came to me.

"Howie, that's the best chicken I've ever had in my life!"

I went back to see Vance.

"Your chicken is a big hit," I told him. "How in the world did you prepare it and what did you season it with?"

"Hell, I don't know," Vance said. "I just threw a bunch of stuff in there until it tasted good to me."

Another incident involving Vance Makanui gave us a good laugh on a squadron flight arranged by the State Department. A lady named Jeannie Bull, now deceased, was in charge at the time of paying for State Department trips. On one of those trips, someone had purchased a bottle of really cheap wine.

"I can't believe they went out and bought a bottle of cheap wine to serve on the airplane," Jeannie said.

She gave me the wine anyway and I just put it on the plane.

One leg of the mission took us from Germany into Paris. Since we were always looking for something to celebrate, we found out one of our flight attendants on board, Steve Estelle, had just had a grandson. We decided to have a party for him at the hotel in Paris.

We were gathering up leftover appetizers on the plane to take to the get-together. Then, I started walking around the plane asking, "Has anyone seen that cheap wine?"

Vance turned to another flight attendant and said, "What is the chief talking about a cheap Hawaiian for?"

I heard it and figured my Long Island accent didn't translate well for him in my question.

"I didn't say 'cheap Hawaiian,' I said 'cheap wine,'" I clarified.

I found out Vance's wife frequently called him a "cheap Hawaiian" and thought I had heard about it and was ribbing him for it.

Chapter Thirty-Seven

A personally memorable event involving a member of the crew took place as the Boeing 747 was being prepared to become Air Force One. The plane had been taken to Wichita, Kansas and being prepped for painting. The interior had been completed so the crew was there to check out the positions on the plane.

While we were there, the decision was made to practice aerially refueling the plane. At the controls was the man considered the co-pilot, Col. Dave Belsito. He was one of the best pilots in the Air Force and flew almost anything the Air Force had. He was the only pilot I know that went from the Air Force directly to the left seat of a JAL airliner as captain, bypassing the first officer position entirely.

Designing the 747 version of Air Force One with the capability of aerial refueling was considered to be a safety issue in the event of a national emergency that meant it was best to keep the president aloft. I was told that it was also a possible money saver since it was estimated it cost a million dollars every time Air Force One had to land and refuel.

With Col. Belsito at the controls, and me on board, we were practicing an aerial refueling behind and slightly below a DC-10. The skill required for this maneuver, both for the pilots and the boom operator, is incredible. It is like threading a needle with a rope.

As the 747 approached the DC-10, the long boom was positioned to be inserted into the refueling port on the nose of the plane. The view from the cockpit looks like the boom is approaching right between your legs.

In the middle of the maneuver I glanced into the cockpit and saw Col. Belsito, who I consider one of the best pilots in the world, sweating bullets.

After the practice refueling was completed, I talked to Col. Belsito.

"You know, you don't have to do this when the president is on board unless you absolutely have to. In fact, you shouldn't even do this when I'm on board."

Despite the capability, I'm unaware of any time Air Force One has ever refueled in flight with the president on board.

While I'm on the subject of fellow crew members, I've saved the best for last. She was an administrative assistant to the presidential pilot and the president on the plane. It was an Air Force position. Her name is Linda, and I married her.

One of Linda's primary duties on Air Force One was to make sure the manifest was correct. That determined who was, and who wasn't, supposed to be on the plane for that trip. Because of last minute changes, her job could, at times, be the equivalent of herding cats.

Prior to a flight, Linda would be in touch with the White House and a manifest would be prepared. Then, she would give a copy to security at the foot of the steps. Whoever came to get on the plane had to be cleared via the manifest.

Linda says the manifest was rarely 100 percent correct. That's because it was a very fluid process due to the ever-changing nature of what is happening in the country and the world. Therefore, who will be traveling with the president on a flight can literally change by the hour.

Having a VIP show up to board the plane, who is not on the manifest, could send Linda running through Air Force one, through a sea of people, in search of a clearance.

This even happened to Sen. Ted Kennedy. He arrived to board Air Force One and his name was not on the manifest. The security man at the base of the steps sees he is not on the manifest and looks to the top of the steps at Linda, who is dressed like she is going to a New York Opera. Imagine the position this put security in to have Sen. Kennedy waiting for permission to board.

After maneuvering her way through the crowd to reach the White House military aide, the aide would call the White House to confirm Sen. Kennedy was supposed to be one the flight. Linda then made her way back through the crowd and to the top of the steps to give security a thumbs-up.

In all probability, someone from Sen. Kennedy's office was on the manifest to make the flight and then he made a last minute decision that he was going, too. These types of scenarios meant the Air Force One manifest was an always changing document.

Mistakes did occasionally happen, as illustrated by the couple who made national news by walking into the White House for a dinner party with the president. It's inevitable something as complex as running a transportation system for the most powerful man in the world would have lots of people involved, meaning a chance of error exists.

Linda describes the process as equivalent to running a stage production.

Chapter Thirty-Eight

Some memorable events took place while we were on overseas trips. Being exposed to different cultures and people led to some interesting events.

Two scary incidents happened on the same trip taking President Carter to the Middle East in January of 1979. On board the flight was an Air Force security policeman whose last name was Tomkiewitz. Everyone called him Tom.

Air Force One had just landed in Saudi Arabia after a trip to Iran. The plane was parked in front of the terminal with the back-up plane quite a distance away, mainly for security reasons. If someone attacked Air Force One the back-up plane would be far enough away to avoid collateral damage and, therefore, still be in service.

Unfortunately, the security guys on Air Force One were not informed that the Saudis planned on giving President Carter a 21-gun salute. These weren't small rifles they were going to use, they were Howitzers.

Tom and the other two members of the security team were standing at the foot of the steps of the plane, facing away from the Saudis, preparing for the salute.

When the Howitzers fired the concussion was incredible. It wasn't just the ear-shattering sounds of the boom, but the ground around the plane literally shook.

BOOM!

Tom jumped straight into the air at least three feet. Before he and the security guy beside him hit the ground their feet were already running.

After the event, the chief of security, who was still aboard Air Force One, asked Tom, "Where were you going?"

"I don't know," Tom said.

As always, while we were in Saudi Arabia, Air Force One security worked shifts at the entry point to the roped-off area around the airplane. It was one guard per shift.

At one of the shift changes, Senior Master Sergeant Reavis arrived at Riyadh Airport escorted by a U.S. Air Force major who was the advance officer for the crew. They were met by a Saudi Arabian security guard.

This very tough-looking guy was wearing sandals and dressed in the traditional Saudi attire of flowing robes and headgear. He was holding an old M-1 rifle.

The major could not convince this guard to give Reavis and him access to the ramp and Air Force One. Nothing he said or did seemed to convince this Saudi guard to let him pass.

Finally, frustrated, the major threw a body block against the Saudi guard and yelled to Reavis, "Run for the airplane!"

Senior Master Sergeant Reavis looked at the major and said, "Sir, you've got to be shittin' me."

Apparently not. They made it to the plane.

Another event involving security guard "Tom" Tomkiewitz happened on a flight to Warsaw, Poland. Tom is a Polish-American and obviously proud to be traveling to the land his family originated from.

In preparation for the president's visit to Poland, the advance team told Polish authorities that they would need a rope line placed around the plane. It is similar to crowd control lines you see in an airport or even a theme park.

However, when we arrived, the rope the Polish government had provided was so thick you could have used it to secure three battleships. There was no way it could be used in something as simple as the supports that held up the rope line.

The security people on Air Force One quickly informed the Polish team the rope was way too thick to be used.

When Tom saw what happened next, he was in shock. Sitting on the ramp, around the plane, was a large contingent of members of the Polish military literally unbraiding the rope in an attempt to get it small enough to use.

Later, Tom called his mother back in the states to tell her he had arrived in Poland. At one point, he told his mother, "Mom, you know those jokes they tell about Poland. We'll they're true."

He then went on to tell her the story of the rope.

Trips to communist countries came with some expectations and some surprises. If we were in China or Russia and stayed in a hotel it was pretty much a given that our hotel room was bugged.

When we were in Russia it was very common to get a phone call from someone offering to bring a woman up to your room.

I was told a story about a 135 crew that was once in Russia and ended up with women in their room. They had a party. It was relayed to me that the CIA was aware of the incident.

When the plane returned to Andrews Air Force Base the base commander was waiting for them. They were all relieved of duty.

If having your hotel room bugged was not bad enough, women who traveled with us to Russia were told to bring shower curtains with them. The curtains in their rooms in Russia would be missing when they checked in. It was obvious they were being bugged and videotaped, too.

The bugging in China was blatantly, and sometimes humorously, obvious. A crewmember could be sitting in their hotel room and simply say, "I sure wish somebody would come pick up my laundry." Within a few minutes there would be a knock on your room door by someone offering to take your clothes to the laundry.

On occasion, we would have a little fun with the knowledge we were always being listened to. Once I said, "You know that stuff they had for breakfast yesterday? It was really good. I sure hope they have that again while we're here."

You can see this one coming from a mile away. The next morning they would have that exact item on the menu.

I recall a trip into China with Secretary of State Henry Kissinger, not long after President Nixon's well-publicized visit to the country. The Chinese government seemed to go out of their way to convince us everyone there was equal. They wanted us to believe everyone in China received the same level of service and that no one was wealthier than another.

Despite their attempts, it was obvious to us there were people who were a bit "more equal" than others. If nothing else, you could tell by their clothes.

My first trip into China got me into a little hot water. Since I had spent some time in Taiwan, I had picked up some Mandarin Chinese. We were on the ground in mainland China and some Chinese were helping us unload baggage from the belly of the plane. When one of them grabbed something we didn't need, I told them not to take that one because it was something we didn't need. The problem became that I said it in Chinese. They immediately labeled me a spy, but nothing became of it.

On another trip to China with Dr. Kissinger, it became rather dicey for a few military security guys on board. After arriving, it was discovered their immunizations were not up to date and they would have to get the shots there in communist China. They were looking mighty pale as they left the airport. It was obvious they were worried just what the Chinese might inject into them.

Chapter Thirty-Nine

I had a fun interchange with Presidential Pilot Col. Danny Barr while we were on a trip to Brussels. We were taken to visit the Battle of Waterloo museum.

In the museum, Col. Barr, Col. Belsito and I walked up some steps to a balcony where you could view a huge mural depicting the battle. We all were scanning the very large artwork.

"Chief, do you see those guys that are taking the hill with their bayonets and fancy uniforms?" Col. Barr asked me. "Do you also see the guy on the horse with the flag?"

"Yes, sir," I said.

"That's the aircraft commander," Col. Barr said.

"Yes, sir," I said. "But, do you see the smoke coming up from the trees in the background, about two miles back?"

"Yes," Col. Barr said.

"That's the flight attendants fixing lunch IF you get back."

Col. Belsito almost fell off of the balcony laughing.

The acquisition of food and beverage became challenging on some overseas missions. Two of those challenges happened on the same trip. We were on a trip to take the then-secretary of the Navy, John Chafee, to Iran.

We were spending the night in Madrid, Spain, where I got word they had requested macaroni salad for one of their meals. We had no macaroni on board.

I wasn't chief steward in those days, but I offered to call protocol in Madrid and order some macaroni and have them cook it in the officer's club. I asked the chief how much I should ask for.

"Have them cook five pounds," he said.

I hopped on the radio, contacted protocol and asked them to have five pounds of macaroni cooked. I advised them we would come out to the club on base and pick it up.

When we arrived to pick up our order, they had prepared not five pounds of macaroni, but fifty pounds of macaroni! They had placed the cooked noodles inside of a plastic bag that they put inside a large cardboard box.

The other steward who had accompanied me to the base asked me, "What do we do with all of this?"

"We take it!" I said.

And we did.

On that same trip, Sec. Chafee requested a bottle of wine. Little did I know I would have to put my old philosophy of Coke bottles in my pockets to work in order to keep a level head in trying to meet such a simple request.

I went to the base officers' club and approached the manager. It became an interesting exchange.

"Sir, I need to buy a bottle of wine for the airplane. It's for the Secretary of the Navy, Chafee," I said.

"We can't sell them over the bar," was the manager's reply.

I tried to appeal to him, explaining the package store was closed and I desperately needed to meet the request of such an important person as the secretary of the Navy. He sent me to talk with an Air Force officer, a captain.

"How can I get a bottle of wine for the secretary?" I asked, after explaining our situation.

"We can't do that," the captain said.

"Well, somehow I've got to make this happen," I said. "Is there anybody that can give me the authority to acquire that bottle of wine?"

"Yeah, the base commander," he said.

I looked him in the eye and asked, "Do you have his number?"

He gave me the bottle of wine.

Chapter Forty

The election of 1992 swung the pendulum in the other political direction and on January 20, 1993, former Arkansas Governor William Jefferson Clinton became the 42nd President of the United States.

As typical protocol during a change of command at the White House, when President Clinton walked on board Air Force One for the first time as commander in chief, he was welcomed by meeting the presidential pilot and the chief flight attendant, the latter being me.

I gave him a flight jacket and welcomed him as "part of the crew."

President Clinton looked the plane over and said, "This is worth the whole campaign."

He liked Air Force One a lot and he liked the crew, too. In fact, at times we, in good nature, claimed he might have liked it too much. During his first term he traveled more than President Bush did and the Bushes had traveled a lot more than President Reagan did.

All of the travel with Clinton led to an inside joke. We would say, "We wanted to make Air Force One a comfortable, professional environment for the president to travel on. We did such a good job we can't get the Clintons off the airplane!"

Air Force One became the Clinton's SUV for a long time and it kept me busy as the chief steward on the plane.

President Clinton was the first president I worked for who was actually a year younger than me. I think our close proximity in age and similar taste in music meant we enjoyed each other's company. I liked him and he liked me. You can just tell when you are around people who like being around you. It had nothing to do with politics since I was actually a non-political person.

He was the only president I worked for that listened to rock and roll. I could certainly relate to that. The previous presidents I served were primarily country fans. The importance of listening to music by President Clinton revealed the one flaw when the new 747 version of Air Force One was designed. It was probably overlooked because listening to music was not commonplace on board by previous presidents.

The problem was there was no way to isolate playing music or other audio into one section of the plane. Whatever was played was piped through the entire aircraft. So, if the president wanted to listen to music, everyone had to hear it and he liked to listen to his rock and roll with the volume cranked up.

The radio operators on Air Force One solved the problem. They purchased two "boom boxes" and had them customized with the Air Force One emblem on them. That way, he could keep one on the plane and take the other one with him to the hotel when he was traveling. The radio operators gave me the units to present to him. I gave them to the president and told him who they were from.

"Sir, I want you to know this is a drastic change," I said after giving him the boom boxes.

"What do you mean?" President Clinton asked.

"In the old days they would have re-wired the whole airplane to take care of this," I said. "It would cost maybe millions!"

"You guys are re-inventing government," Clinton said. "I like it!"

People who have been around President Clinton frequently comment on his intelligence. I believe they are right. I would see him complete an entire *New York Times* crossword puzzle in 15 minutes, while carrying on business at the same time.

It was obvious he subscribed to Total Quality Management concepts. In fact, we once had a guest on Air Force One who was reading a book on TQM. President Clinton took notice and told him, "You know, I brought that into Arkansas politics. That's the way to go."

Clinton's style would, unintentionally on occasion, create some challenges for the flight attendants. That usually occurred when he was very busy and had several guests on board. He would try to fit everything in.

I recall one such occasion well.

"Howie, you know I'm busy today and I don't have a lot of time to entertain these people," Clinton said. "So, what I would like to do is invite them into the conference room and I'll eat with them there."

He didn't realize it, but that created a logistical problem for us responsible for feeding people in the plane. The meal preparation and planning was planned ahead and split between two separate galleys on Air Force One. The galleys were located on opposite ends of the plane. This change meant the people who were sitting in the back of the plane were now up front and yet we still had to feed them out of the back galley. It just made the operation not as smooth as usual. But, we made it work.

On a later flight, he came to me with a similar request.

"You know I'm busy, so I'm not going to be able to go back and have lunch with my guests," he said to me. "Why don't you just bring them up to the conference room and let them eat and I'll go back and visit with them briefly when I can."

This time I knew some of his staff was already working in the conference room and they had material spread out around the room. So, I decided to see if I could put the president's interest in TQM to work.

"Sir, I can do that," I began. "But, your guests are sitting in the VIP guest area and they seem pretty comfortable. We could just leave them right there, feed them, and then you can go back and visit them at your pleasure."

President Clinton looked at me and said, "You're the chief. You know what you're doing."

He was smart. He was very much aware that since I made the recommendation, I had to make sure it worked. It was Total Quality Management at its best.

There was a fine line on Air Force One between remaining professional at all times and in interacting on a personal level with the president and his family. It could be the kiss of death if anyone on the crew or staff felt you were too close to the president.

However, if people truly enjoy the company of each other, it's hard not to form some type of bond. The chief steward during President Reagan's days was close to him. They cared very much for each other. To this day, when Nancy Reagan sees Charlie Palmer she is going to give him a hug.

While I worked hard to make sure it wasn't outwardly obvious, President Clinton and I had a good relationship and that meant he was comfortable in saying just about anything to me, and vice-versa. He would frequently joke with me and make all kinds of comments.

Once, I was nearby on the plane when he was reading a book about President Kennedy.

"Howie, according to John F. Kennedy, if he didn't have a woman at least once every three days he wasn't worth a crap."

"Sounds good to me, sir," I said.

I'm sure that story instantly reminded anyone reading it of the reputation he had as far as women were concerned. He did joke about it with us.

When you compared the Air Force One crew that we built when I became chief steward on the plane, it was practically a rainbow coalition of diversity compared to what it had been in the past.

On my crew we had women, African Americans and Hispanic Americans serving on board. That was quite a change considering that, not too many years prior, women were specifically prohibited from serving as flight attendants in the Air Force. The thinking was to avoid even the hint of impropriety on missions between them and the passengers they were serving.

In those days the word was that there was a regulation which stated in order to be a flight attendant in the Air Force you had to have at least one testicle.

By the time President Clinton was on board, that had changed a great deal. We had a fantastic crew. It was like an on-board Dale Carnegie course. Plus, no one was chosen for the crew on board to meet any quotas. They were picked because they were good at what they did. Now that we had women on board, the president joked on several occasions to several people that I was hiding them from him.

"Howie, you're keeping those women from me," he said once.

"What do you mean, sir?"

"I haven't seen them. They're usually up in the front galley."

"I like to rotate everybody," I said. "I don't like to keep everybody in one place all the time. I like to keep them proficient all the way around. Every couple of trips, we rotate."

"I was just wondering why you are keeping the women from me," he said.

This became a running gag, another one of those MASH moments on board. We worked on serious missions that kept us all on the edge. This escapism was a welcome distraction.

On a later flight a foreign dignitary was a guest of President Clinton. I happened to be working in their area of the plane when the president pointed at me.

"See that guy over there?" he asked his guest. "He's keeping the women from me."

"No, sir, I rotate everybody," I said, smiling.

During another mission, my deputy chief steward, Timmy, was on a flight with President Clinton. When they returned, Timmy tracked me down.

"The president told me to tell you that if you bring the women up front he'll promote you and give you a pay raise," Timmy said.

"What did you say to him?" I asked.

"I said, 'Sir, with all respect, he is as high as he can go and if you give him a pay raise you will have to give us all one.'"

"Good answer," I said.

Timmy said the president responded by throwing his hands up and walking away in mock disgust.

Chapter Forty-One

When the tabloid-style stories about President Clinton's personal life began to fill the news, I confess to being surprised. I knew many powerful men had skeletons in their closet, but, in the past, the media shied away from those stories. This time it was all over the news. While I usually avoid talking about the press and news when I was on board, I did briefly get into an exchange on a flight with David Gergen of the White House Communications Agency.

Gergen, who now serves as senior political analyst for CNN, had served almost as many presidents as I did. He had been an advisor to the president in the Nixon, Ford and Reagan administrations and was serving in the same capacity with President Clinton when we had our discussion.

"Why is the press doing this?" I asked Gergen. "Usually, they wouldn't talk about things like that."

I will never forget Gergen's response.

"Well, nowadays the press is nothing but a bunch of granola-eating tight asses," he said.

I believe all reporters have a bias. When a reader or viewer considers a reporter as a liberal, the reporter is probably further left than the reader thinks. When they are moderate, they are probably further left than that. When someone considers a reporter to be more conservative, the reporter is probably further to the left than the reader believes. The reason is because of the environment they live and work in.

Whatever anyone thinks or believes about President Clinton, I never saw any interaction between him and his family that did not indicate anything but a mutual respect and love for each other. It was obvious they enjoyed each other's company very much.

People certainly have the capacity to be good actors around others, but that becomes very difficult to pull off when you are tired and under enormous stress. I personally witnessed the reality of the Clintons interacting with each other during such a time. It was when the president's mother died.

She was very close to her son and we could see that when she flew with us on Air Force One. There was an enormous mutual love and respect between them and she was very proud of her son serving as President of the United States. She was a character and she enjoyed Air Force One a lot. We tried to treat her as a mom should be treated. It was a tough time for the president when she passed away.

President Clinton returned to Arkansas for three days to attend the events around his mother's funeral. It was, like for any of us dealing with a death in the family, an exhausting and emotionally-draining time. When he returned to Washington, it was aboard a Gulfstream that had been designated as Air Force One for this private, family trip. Another steward, Timmy, was acting as a flight attendant on that trip.

When the Gulfstream landed at Andrews Air Force Base, it taxied up to the tarmac where the 747 was waiting. He literally walked off of the Gulfstream and onto the 747, which was waiting to take him to Moscow, Russia for a summit.

Not only was he just leaving his mother's funeral and facing a long flight and event in Moscow, but arrangements had already been agreed to for Ted Koppel to originate an episode of ABC News' *Nightline* from Air Force One.

When President Clinton walked on board, Ted Koppel was waiting and the interview began. Koppel expressed sympathy for the loss of the president's mother and asked him about the funeral.

"I understand at your mother's funeral, you did not speak," Koppel said.

"That's right," Clinton responded. "I thought it was time for a son to be a son."

I have always admired his response.

Despite the emotional and physical fatigue after attending his mother's funeral, President Clinton completed the segment with Ted Koppel on *Nightline,* including a walk-through of the plane with the camera rolling.

Right after the Koppel interview we were ready to begin the flight to the Moscow summit. It was very late and the decision was made to wake the president up an hour-and-a-half before arriving in Russia so that he could get ready and prepare. It would also give me that much time to have his clothes out and be dressed before he met the press in Moscow after landing. That meant he was only going to get two-and-a-half hours sleep.

There are two couches on Air Force One in the president's private state room that pull out into comfortable beds. His wife, Hillary, was on board and they were using both couches.

When I entered to wake them up it was 3:00 a.m., Washington time, and the time our bodies were adapted to.

I went into their room and leaned slightly on the president. He groaned a little.

"Sir, I hate to do this," I said.

"Well, don't do it," President Clinton said.

We had a comfortable enough relationship that I could say things to the president that no one ever would in a public setting.

"Sir, it's time to get your butt up and go to work."

I glanced over towards Mrs. Clinton and she was peeking out of her covers with a semi-smile on her face.

"Don't laugh, you're next," I said to her.

Before I awoke the president and Hillary Clinton, I already had crewmembers on board getting their coffee ready and the first lady's hairdresser prepared to do her hair. Mrs. Clinton's mother was on board and I woke her up, too.

Despite their sleep deprivation and my barking orders to get everything ready on the approach to Moscow, I witnessed a family getting along better than my family did getting ready for church on a Sunday morning. They were not trying to show off for me. This was the way they were in real life, behind the scenes. They interacted in a positive way even under duress.

I intervened to make a change in protocol as a result of this trip. President Clinton told me what he wanted to wear. I had the suitcases out but didn't have a clue where the valet had packed what he wanted. The valet was traveling on the back-up plane. Following that mission I made sure the valet was where he needed to be. Despite the time our body clocks were working under and all the details needing to be accomplished we got them ready and out of the plane on time.

On this trip and others, I got the chance to see who the Clintons really were. I saw them obviously appreciating each other's gifts and talents. I saw how they were with Chelsea and the times they all three played cards together. I also got to see Mrs. Clinton being a mother. They all really enjoyed each other's company very much.

Hillary Clinton was aggressive and decisive, but she also had a great sense of humor.

I remember when she and her staff were on board in the state room working on her proposed health care program. I opened the door to see if they needed anything and Mrs. Clinton said, "Oh, it's just Howie. Don't worry about him."

Did she ever get mad at her husband? Absolutely. But, I witnessed mostly a positive interaction between them.

Chapter Forty-Two

Next to the negative press regarding President Clinton's personal life, another one of the biggest stories in the media during his term in office came during what would definitely be a non-event for you and me – a haircut. In this case, it was the President of the United States getting a haircut in Air Force One on the ramp of Los Angeles International Airport. In my opinion, the president was backed into a corner in this incident.

When someone new enters the White House, regardless of their political party, there is frequently an outcry to bring fresh blood onto the staff and not use as many of the "old guard." However, in the case of the haircut, an experienced staff member could have prevented this from becoming the embarrassment it did to the president. They would have learned from the proverbial "been there-done that" what works and what can end up being a nightmare. After all, most of us learn more from our mistakes than we do from our successes.

President Clinton made the trip to California to attend a major fundraising event for the Democrat party. The appearance of the president took place at the home of a very wealthy donor. As the story was told to me, someone approached President Clinton while he was there and said, "Sir, we're going to get you the best barber in Los Angeles to come out and cut your hair."

The person offering the haircut was obviously a big contributor to the Democrats and was trying to impress the president by arranging something personal and special for him. When you have someone giving huge amounts to the cause, what do you say? There was apparently no experienced staff member around who could have headed off this logistical issue at the pass. A member of the old-guard staff could have jumped in and said, "Thank you for the generous offer but, considering the president's schedule, we'll have to pass."

The crew, including me, remained at LAX awaiting the president's return to Air Force One. I got a phone call.

"Howie, there is a gentleman coming out to the plane and he's going to cut the president's hair. His name is Cristophe."

I said I would make the arrangements to get him through security and on the plane.

When a white limousine pulled up, I happened to be at the top of the steps. A gentleman got out of the limo. He was about six feet tall with sandy blonde hair and wearing cowboy boots, blue jeans, a white linen shirt and a jean jacket. The flight engineers, who were standing with me, were both very curious about this barber all decked out in cowboy attire.

"Wonder what we're going to get here?" one flight engineer asked.

"I just heard he's supposed to be the best barber in L.A.," I said.

As this barber, who went by one name, boarded Air Force One I noticed he was carrying a Louis Vuitton case. I had once been told you could tell a real Louis Vuitton by the examining the lettering. If the "L" or "V" had any stitching in them it was a knockoff. This guy looked like he had the real thing. This meant this guy's portable barber supply bag was worth about $1,500!

The moment I spoke with Cristophe I noticed he had a French accent. He told me he was born in Belgium and grew up in the French Riviera.

After the incident at LAX, the media reported Cristophe got $200 a haircut. However, he told me he was paid $500 per haircut. He said he had not had a full day off in six months. So, this guy was doing pretty doggone good cutting hair!

Cristophe said he got the call to come cut President Clinton's hair while he was in wine country with a friend. They had flown him in to LAX just to cut the president's hair.

"Sir, if you make $500 a haircut, and you haven't had a day off in six months, then you are going to be in the president's high tax bracket," I said.

We both laughed.

While we were waiting for the president to return to the plane I gave him a show-and-tell of Air Force One. After the tour, we decided the state room would be the best place for the president's haircut. To prepare, I did what most of us would do if we were going to cut one of our own children's hair. I got a sheet to put around his neck to keep hair from getting on his clothes.

Just after we had prepared the state room a large number of people arrived for a tour of the plane. They were attendees from the big fundraiser. We had never had this large of a group tour the plane my entire time serving on Air Force One. It was something obviously arranged as a thank you to the major donors at the event. Normally, we would have between four to eight people for a tour. This group numbered over 40.

Having that many people on board is a security problem. The rule was we had to have one crewmember observing every two people touring the plane. So, we had crew placed all over the plane to meet the requirement.

As these wealthy donors boarded the plane and passed the state room, where I was located with Cristophe, it was obvious the majority of them knew this barber who was about to cut the president's hair. Most of them called him by name.

After the donors had their tour President Clinton arrived and received his haircut. It crossed my mind while Cristophe was doing his thing that I wonder what a guy who gets $500 a haircut received in tips. It was typical L.A. because Cristophe got paid such a high price for a haircut not because of haircuts but because of who he was. It was the barber version of wearing designer clothes.

The president's haircut hit the national news that night. It wasn't because of who did the haircut but because of what the event did to traffic around the airport due to the security protocol surrounding Air Force One. It meant certain roadways were closed, traffic detours were in place and other aircraft were not allowed in the vicinity of the plane.

So, the haircut meant some airplanes had a delay in getting airborne and there was some traffic backup around LAX. It wasn't as bad as portrayed in the press, but it was noticeable.

The media stories gave the impression President Clinton was holding up traffic around one of the busiest airports in the country simply so he could get something as vain as an expensive haircut. The truth was he was livid when he found out what had happened.

In reality, it was a series of unfortunate events that led to the haircut he had not even asked for, which led to traffic delays around LAX. If an experienced staff member would have intervened back at the fundraiser the entire event would have never happened. President Clinton was very upset over the decisions that were made.

Clinton was the type of president who preferred to travel in a Suburban rather than a limousine. So, this haircut, and the associated problems surrounding it, did not portray who he was or the image he wanted to project in his position.

An example of the simple side of Clinton is the fact he frequently played golf on the course located at Andrews Air Force Base rather than at some country club setting.

After playing a round on base, he would usually want to take a shower and change clothes before leaving Andrews. In those scenarios, I was usually asked to meet the president at the Air Force One office because he knew me and that simply made the affair simpler.

Early in his first term, he played a round on the Andrews course and I met him at the Air Force One hangar afterwards. He requested to take a shower. As we made our way towards the office, I showed him the many photos of former presidents hanging in the area. He seemed to feel very comfortable and enjoyed the tour.

When I escorted President Clinton to the shower I forgot to brief him on a unique aspect of the shower in the Air Force One office area. The shower was located quite some distance from the hot water heater meaning it took quite a while for the hot water to actually make its way to the shower.

After he had been in the shower for a while, I heard him shout, "Do I get hot water?"

"It's coming, sir!" I said.

Chapter Forty-Three

Steve Lominac was the number three flight attendant on Air Force One during my tenure as chief steward during the Clinton days. Steve and I began what would become a running gag with President Clinton for years.

It started on a trip to Florida where the president was making some campaign fundraising appearances. I saw his schedule and he had no time off to do anything. So, knowing he was in ear shot, I turned to Steve.

"Hey, Steve, did you bring your clubs?"

Before Steve could respond, President Clinton said, "You guys going to play golf?"

"Yes, sir!"

"I'll be damn," the president said. "They can't give me four hours off to play golf. I'm down here raising all this money and you guys are playing golf."

"Yes, sir, we're playing golf," I said.

"Where are you playing?" he asked.

"We're playing at Doral."

"You're playing at Doral?!?!" he exclaimed.

Doral Golf Resort in Miami is considered one of the top three courses in Florida.

"Yes, sir," I said. "And we're playing there free because we know you!"

After I retired, the man who was deputy chief steward, Timmy, took my place on Air Force One. Timmy told me about one interchange he had with the president after I left. President and Mrs. Clinton were talking with him when I became the subject.

"Is Howie still in North Carolina?" the president asked.

"Not only is Howie in North Carolina, but Steve is in North Carolina, too," Timmy said. "They both live on a golf course and Steve works on the golf course. So, they both get to play free golf."

Timmy told me President Clinton threw his hands up and said, "Those guys!

Slightly less than two months after that interchange, one of my airport customers in North Carolina, who lives in Elmira, New York, told me the Clintons were coming to his home because Hillary Clinton was being inducted into a hall of fame for New York women. She was getting ready to run for the Senate and he had donated property where they were going to build the hall of fame.

"Howie, since President Clinton is coming to my house and you worked for him and know him, what should I say to him?" he asked.

"Do you have a golf ball?" I asked him. Then, I proceeded to tell him what to say to President Clinton.

During the first-class reception for Hillary Clinton in Elmira, the host walked up to President Clinton and handed him a golf ball.

"This is from Howie and Steve in North Carolina and they say hello," the host said. "They're both living on a golf course and they get to play free golf."

Clinton took the golf ball and said, "I've been hearing that all over the world!"

After I had retired and settled into my new job at Cape Fear Regional Jetport, my niece, Rachel McPherson, graduated from Peace College in Raleigh and went to work for a big corporation in Boston.

Mrs. Clinton ended up in Boston for a fundraiser and Rachel somehow got into the event. She ended up meeting Hillary and introduced herself by saying, "I'm Howie Franklin's niece."

A secret service agent I knew sent me an e-mail about their meeting and said, "That's the longest I've ever seen Mrs. Clinton stop and talk with someone who wasn't giving her $10,000."

I was interviewed by the *Charlotte Observer* once and asked about my opinion of Hillary Clinton. She saw it and sent me a very kind, personally-written note.

My oldest daughter, Cheri Nichols, was in Georgetown, South Carolina, once when President Clinton was campaigning for his wife there. As he was walking through the crowd, my daughter shouted, "My dad used to work for you on Air Force One!"

The president slowed and asked, "Who is your dad?"

"Howie Franklin," my daughter said.

"Stop the parade!" Clinton said, as he walked up to my daughter. "You know I love that guy."

"He loves you, too," my daughter said.

It's hard for me to tell that story to friends without tearing up.

He wrote me a handwritten note after he saw my daughter.

Later, on the campaign trail for Mrs. Clinton, he ended up coming to Lumberton, North Carolina. I contacted Steve Lominac and told him we should drive to Lumberton to see him.

"Let's go see him, for him," I said. "I think he'd get a kick out of it. It would be like a teacher having two old students show up to say hello."

They had Steve and I positioned near the limousine as he exited Air Force One and made his way greeting people along the rope line. When he saw us, he was noticeably happy to see us.

"I love you guys," he said.

Chapter Forty-Four

Things have changed since my days as a flight attendant on Air Force One. When I was on board, there were a total of 18 flight attendants who worked the president's plane. Now, there are 30.

In my day, the entire staff and crew numbered 36 people. Now, that number is 330.

One of the reasons for that is the plane now operates under squadron flight rules. That means everyone is under strict duty time requirements. So, days working 52 hours in a row, like a flight with President Carter that took him from Washington to Georgia, back to Washington, and then to Germany and back to Washington, no longer happens with one crew.

There was no one star on the crew of Air Force One. It was 100 percent team work.

Our number one mission on Air Force One was to provide secure and safe transportation for the president. We also wanted to provide all the services the White House provided on the plane and give him a relaxed atmosphere on board.

The entire crew I worked with on Air Force One understood attitude and good service. I'm in no doubt that any Air Force One crewmember could give an amazing course on good service and good customer relations.

I've been retired from the president's plane for many years now and have become entrenched in my new position as airport director at Cape Fear Regional Jetport near Southport and Oak Island in North Carolina.

As if I haven't had a wonderful life already, I was surprised a few years ago when the airport authority renamed the airport where I work. It's now Cape Fear Regional Airport at Howie Franklin Field. Not bad for a Long Island boy who once made tips pulling a wagon of luggage for the rich and famous on Fire Island, huh?

I have come a long way from training at Lackland Air Force Base, but still put those proverbial Coke bottles to use on occasion.

My new work keeps me busy and I put the people skills I learned working at Talisman Yacht club right on through serving five presidents to use almost every day. The staff and I at the airport use those skills to serve the pilots, passengers and guests that visit what we call our "little airport with the big heart."

Believe it or not, I could keep right on going talking about the great people I've met and fantastic places I've seen. However, my phone is ringing so it's back to work.

"Cape Fear Regional Jetport, Howie Franklin speaking. What can we do to make your day better?"

Co-Author's Note: In addition to the name change of the airport, where Howie serves as director, to Cape Fear Regional Airport at Howie Franklin Field, the official FAA instrument approach plate to Runway 5 at the airport has a waypoint named HOWWE in his honor. You can see it under the magnifying glass in the graphic below.

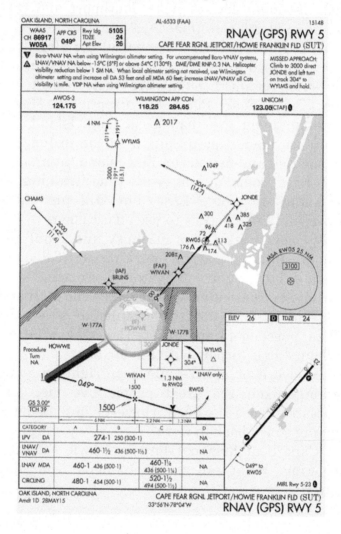

CPSIA information can be obtained at www.ICGtesting.com
Printed in the USA
BVOW08*0346101215

429728BV00003B/13/P